My Esenin:

Anatomy

of a Folktale

Selected poems

Compiled and translated by Olga Zolotarev

Published by London Mists Press
londonmists@gmail.com

A CIP record of this book is available from the British Library.

Cover photo colourized by © Olga Shirnina (Instagram:
color_by_klimbim)

Cover design: Dmitry Zolotarev

Illustrations: Anna Yakusheva (Instagram: jakuseva.anna)

ISBN: 978-1-5272-3838-1

For my all-time favourite poet who berhymed the prose of life.

Поэты не рождаются случайно.
Они летят на землю с высоты.
Их жизнь окружена глубокой тайной,
Хотя они открыты и просты.
Глаза таких таинственных посланцев
Всегда печальны и верны мечте.
И в хаосе проблем их души вечно светят тем
Мирам, что заблудились в темноте.

Игорь Тальков 'Памяти Виктора Цоя'

ξ

Poets are transcendent human beings.
They fly to Earth from somewhere high above.
Their lives are nothing short of an enigma,
Although they may be humble and homespun.
The eyes of those occult and mystic envoys
Are always sad and true to their dream.
And in the maze of life,
Their souls are shedding guiding light
On all those lost and stumbling in the dark.

Igor Talkov, 'In Memory of Viktor Tsoy'*

"He had youth, beauty, genius. Dissatisfied with these gifts, his gallant spirit sought the impossible. He destroyed his young and beautiful body but his spirit will live for ever in the hearts of the Russian people and in the hearts of all who love poetry."

Isadora Duncan

All views and opinions expressed in this book are strictly those of the author and are speculative in nature; they simply offer the author's arguable interpretation of all the literature they have read on the subject to date. These views and opinions, as well as some historical facts and references are there solely for the purpose of putting Sergei Esenin's life and work in a literary context, giving the reader a bigger picture and facilitating acquaintance with his poetic legacy.

Extracts from various other poems and books, included in the narration and marked with *, were also translated by the author.

Esenin's complete set of works comprises seven volumes, so this selection is not a true representation of his multiplex topics and philosophy. It does, however, feature Esenin's most iconic and recognisable pieces (in the author's opinion). Those who prefer more upbeat, feel-good poetry might be interested in Esenin's early and less-known verse that may be found in English online or in print.

CONTENTS

ACKNOWLEDGEMENTS

Massive thanks are due to my favourite turbo toddler, George – for bearing with his mummy while she played 'the next big thing in writing'; above all, to my own mother Anna Lesyk, whose vocation is teaching Russian Literature to people of all ages – for allowing me to 'play' with her books as a child; something that made me the book-savvy and a passionate bilingual that I am today; to extremely gifted artist and illustrator Anna Yakusheva - for exquisite and original art capturing the essence of Esenin's folktale; to Andrew Hall, Olivia Rolfs, and my favourite Chekhov fan, Heather Griffin – for their comprehensive editing efforts and invaluable improvements to the style and content; and last but not least – to all my former teachers of English, both in hometown of Nefteyugansk and at the Nevsky Institute for Language and Culture, St. Petersburg, Russia – for encouraging me to always strive for excellence and never rest on my laurels; and for providing the academic backbone of all my subsequent linguistic achievements. I am honoured to name and fame these wonderful people here:

Svetlana Matviiv and Olga Arapova – teachers of English at Secondary School №10, Nefteyugansk, Tyumen region, Western Siberia;
The amazing staff at the Nevsky Institute for Language and Culture (2001 - 2006):

i

Ekaterina Nikolaeva, Olga Bychek, Yulia Ulyanova, Eugene Pushkarev, Julia Rastvorova, Tatiana Kalikina, Nina Petrova, and Margarita Kabakchi – English Language teachers (grammar, listening and conversation);

Larissa Gurochkina, Igor Arkhipov, Ksenia Guzeeva, Tamara Kazakova, and Tatiana Sallier – acclaimed lecturers of English Language and Translation Studies from St Petersburg State University and Herzen State Pedagogical University;

with *special thanks* to the heads of the International Relations and Philological Faculties of the Nevsky Institute for Language and Culture (2001-2006) - Marina Dibrova and Galina Ishchuk respectively.

ABOUT THE BOOK

First things first, if, like myself, you are one of those no-nonsense individuals who desperately want to believe in the law of attraction, and in the power of the mind to create reality, yet always need some kind of tangible proof to that end, this book is *it*.

It may not have been the best time to start writing a book – having just had a baby and being busy adjusting to a new life of three 'No's' (no wine, no coffee, no sleep) – yet I somehow knew that this was long overdue. And since we Russians never take the easy way of doing things, I kissed a mental goodbye to what little sleep remained and gave this project the Gagarin treatment (Poehali!). In other words, the laborious work commenced.

Overall it has taken me nineteen years to bring Sergei Esenin's particular poetic qualities to life in the English language, from the ephemeral dream to the finished product. Without blowing my own trumpet, I must say it has been well worth the wait.

I have always believed Esenin to be rather underestimated by the international Russian-speaking community, both as a poet and a citizen - for the same reason that makes his work so outstanding: he is timeless, non-main stream, and he certainly doesn't fit neatly into any current political or cultural trend. He is a legend, and all legendary things are known to turn into myths, gradually sinking into the alcove of people's collective unconscious.

Abroad, Esenin is not typically seen as among the first rank of twentieth-century Russian poets, but he is historically important. And while he has achieved some degree of posthumous celebrity – mainly as the wild, good-looking husband of the free-spirited American dancer Isadora Duncan – rarely, if ever, does his name come up in Western European culture on its own. Equally, it will hardly be the first name to come to mind of an English-speaker talking about Russian poetry. And that was something I intended to correct in this book.

Sergei Esenin is important to us Russians for a number of reasons. No less because his name has always been associated with patriotism. It must be noted here that the word 'patriot' seems to have acquired rather negative connotations in the contemporary Russian context, invariably drawing smirks and criticism from the home-grown liberal crowd.

It is evident, however, that when related to the works of this self-styled 'last poet of wooden Russia', patriotism appears to represent something entirely different, namely a form of national self-awareness in its purest form.

Esenin loved his homeland dearly, and this love was manifested in an unconditional devotion to his native tongue, native landscape, Slavic heritage and folklore. Just as charity begins at home in English culture, so does patriotism in Esenin's world. When one loves the little neck of the woods they hail from and wants to see or make it a better place, that's what grown-up, healthy patriotism is really about (as opposed to a familiar dissident mentality of moaning about a regime from the comfort of one's new, foreign home). And that's why Esenin is in my opinion, an example of what modern day Russian patriots should be like: neither flag-wavers nor oppositionists, just *Esenians*[1].

It is no surprise that at home, in Russia itself, the poet is respected, and indeed revered, by people of different assertions, walks of life, and outlooks.

Esenin has always held a truly mass, sort of fairy-tale appeal for his vernacular, yet complex poetic style; and this appeal is unique. His legacy needs no political context or a favourable ideological climate in order to exist and be celebrated. His verse is beyond trends and national geopolitical ambition. This is all for one simple reason: he is a living legend, and his verse is life itself. It lives, breathes, and pulls at the invisible strings deep inside, making you sad, or peaceful, or inspired. Whether it's through a unique choice of words or the way Esenin put them together, his poems are packed full of energy

---

[1] Term coined by the author.

waiting to be released into the hearts and minds of his readers.

***

Previous attempts have been made to translate Esenin's work into English, with varied success. I feel privileged to have been able to add to the truly international effort. Nothing would make me happier than knowing that more people are going to be swept away by his specific rhyming style, relatively simple yet engaging diction, and delicate nuances of authentic imagery that are so reflective of the Russian life pre and post the Great October Revolution. Using the familiar mathematical terms, Sergei Esenin equals the elusive Russian spirit, and to understand him would perhaps be to understand Russia itself.

I have used my extensive linguistic knowledge and skills, accumulated over years of study and translation work, to deliver my version of Esenin's 'Best of' to the rest of the world. I would like to think that my effort will give his poetic heritage a second life and a well-deserved 'breakthrough' on foreign soil. And to the readers - a glimpse of his range and some of the features that made him one of the most hailed Russian poets of all time, not least during a Soviet ban on his work (imposed shortly after his death and lifted in the 1960s).

***

I wanted this book to be a treat for poetry lovers in general and Russian poetry fans in particular. But given the bilingual nature of the text (the translations are presented along with the original poems), this book may also prove useful to those interested in learning, practicing, or honing their Russian or English language skills, as well as the tricky art of poetry translation - which brings me to my next point.

How are my translations different from any other samples taken from Esenin or any other poet or writer? I don't claim to be an expert in translating poetry, and I cannot speak for any other translations out there, but one thing I know for sure: poetry can be a real nightmare for translators, and there will always be a temptation to cut corners by resorting to prose. This is mainly because the theory of translation teaches us that one should translate the meaning behind the words rather than the actual words. And meanings are not known to rhyme.

Yet I always knew that if I ever attempted to translate Esenin's poetry, prose would not be an option. Putting his verse into prose is a poetic crime.

As Esenin's poetry is very visual, I made this imagery my starting point. Then I just let my linguistic hunch and imagination roam free in search of the best possible poetic analogies to use in English while trying to preserve Esenin's original style and rhythm, which are unique for every poem. I would like to believe that being a native Russian speaker only played to my advantage here.

Apart from the selected poems, the book offers a cursory overview of Esenin's life and major career milestones.

***

At one point in 2018 (with Russia-UK relations hitting new political lows by the hour), halfway through the project, I began to doubt whether my efforts were worth it. I was no longer sure if the subject would be of any interest to the general English speaking public. Then I remembered my last trip to a bookshop on my local High Street, and the cornucopia of titles and subject matters, and I reconsidered. Surely, if there was a demand for books on cat selfies and the art of tippling, then my work was bound to find a dedicated audience too.

I hope you enjoy reading it.

ABOUT THE AUTHOR

Growing up, I was surrounded by the finest examples of Russian literature, including the master of poetic parable, Alexander Pushkin[2], and Soviet poetry idols, such as Evgeniy Evtushenko, Leonid Filatov, and Igor Talkov; these figures pretty much shaped my literary taste and, in a way, my outlook on life. And the poetic genius of Sergei Esenin has always topped that list.

My first ever attempt at translating Esenin was in the penultimate year of high school. Nineteen years ago precisely. I remember coming back home overwhelmed with emotion – we had had a lesson on Sergei Esenin in

---

[2] Apart from prose and poetry, Alexander Pushkin wrote children's tales rich in allegories and symbols pertaining to ancient Slavic folklore. Some modern day philologists and scholars hold that Pushkin intentionally dressed ancient Slavic myths and belief as folktales so that certain knowledge and wisdom of our Slavic ancestors could be preserved and passed onto future generations.

our Russian Literature class earlier that day. I just remember badly wanting to cry– so sad had I felt for Esenin, having just learnt the story of his life and death. I then took a small volume by him from my mother's book-case and was glued to it until bedtime. I even couldn't be bothered with my homework that night. I simply couldn't concentrate on anything else, the heart-rending lines from his poems resounding in my head.

I distinctly recall crying my heart out over one poem in particular – *'Letter to Mother'* (written towards the end of his life), as in it he wrote:

> *I'll be back when our luscious garden*
> *Blooms all white in marvellous spring glow.*
> *Only, please, don't wake me up at sunrise,*
> *Like you did those eight summers ago.*[3]

Reading those lines for the first time, while already knowing all too well how tragically Esenin's life had ended, was a surreal, almost heart-stopping experience.

---

[3] Extracts from all poems, included in the body of the book and marked with *, were also translated by the author.

Sometime later I translated my very first poem of his into English – *"Nowadays I can't scatter this sadness..."* – and I promised myself (although 'promised' is a bit strong; rather I mused) that one day I would do all of them – well, most of them – for the rest of the world to weep over.

I couldn't know then that one day I would move to the UK. I didn't even know which university I would go to the following year, for that matter. So, naturally, life found a way to occupy my mind with other things, and kept it occupied until about two years ago, when I accidentally came across that original translation in my school papers (I'm a sentimental type that has a school/university keepsake box stashed under my bed). Totally embarrassed by the standard of my English back then, I made a few hasty corrections and produced a new version, which eventually led me to create this book. And thus I closed the circle.

***

A lot has happened to me since that fateful translation experiment. I graduated from university (cum laude), worked as a freelance translator and interpreter/tour guide in St Petersburg (my academic alma mater) for a short while, moved to the UK and (for a longer while) got trapped in the perfectly boring office and admin world – something I can now say I have always been overqualified for.

But one day a friend of mine asked me to read through her college essay, and then another one, and then a few more. So began my editing and proofreading hobby-turned-part-time-career.

Today I'm proud to have quite a few large-scale translating and copyediting projects under my belt, including the translation of an interview by an up-and-coming Russian abstract painter for an upscale international art magazine.

Writing and translating is my passion. And this book is, by far, the best thing I have achieved in those realms – even if I do say so myself.

INTRODUCTION

Twentieth-century Russian poetry gave the world the titans of Alexander Blok, Vladimir Mayakovsky, Anna Akhmatova, and Boris Pasternak to name but a few. They were all legends in their own right. They all, in their own unique way, encapsulated the spirit of the époque. But none did it better than the one and only Sergei Esenin – the hopeless romantic, self-confessed troublemaker and arguably, Alexander Pushkin's rightful successor.

> *Daydreaming of your mighty power*
> *That has defined our Russian fate,*
> *I'm at your feet, in Tverskoy bulvar,*
> *Talking to you inside my head.*
>
> *With fair-hair, almost chalky,*
> *My life now but a wild tale.*
> *You, Alexander, were a heartthrob,*
> *As I'm a hooligan today.*
>
> *(«To Pushkin», 1924)**

Esenin's poetry has had people talking ever since his first published book of poems. To look at his early, then later work, and everything in-between, one would be surprised to learn that it had been written by the same person. Not suffering from a split personality disorder, Esenin still managed to match the unmatchable in the grand scheme of things. Only Esenin could get away with being a pious sinner, a faithful womaniser, a gentle cynic, a forward-minded retrograde, and a city slicking country boy. Spiritual dualism is generally considered a Russian national trait (think of the double-headed eagle on the Russian Federation coat of arms) and is one of the reasons why I thought no other poet represented the Russian spirit better.

In Russia itself, Esenin is not referred to as anything other than the people's poet. This might be because there is something about his work that every Russian generation can relate to. And everyone can find something in his poems to be grabbed by.

Out of the cohort of extremely gifted early

twentieth-century Russian poets, also referred to collectively as the poets of the Silver Age[4], Esenin stood out for a variety of (mostly) good reasons. He had pro vita become known for his melodious rhyming style and gift of song. No one before him had had so many of their poems put to music. The resulting songs are enchanting examples of Russian folk culture. Some of them were perpetuated in film (such as '*The Elusive Avengers*', *USSR, 1966*); some were revived in the '90s by a folk band *Zolotoe Koltso* (Golden Ring).

Esenin wrote poems about literally everything. Once he had started, he wouldn't stop until the night before he died by all accounts[5] . His repertoire featured every poetic style possible: children's verse, romantic ballads (early work and cycle of poems '*Persian Motifs*'), historical pieces ('*Pugachev*' and '*Land of Scoundrels*'), and rough 'street' writing full of expletives (cycle of poems '*Tavern Moscow*').

---

[4] Silver Age - a term traditionally applied by Russian philologists to the last decade of the nineteenth century and first two or three decades of the twentieth century. It was an exceptionally creative period in the history of Russian poetry, on par with the Golden Age a century earlier. (Wikipedia)
[5] Poem 'Goodbye, my friend, it's time to leave', 211

Largely autobiographical, his works covered a wide range of topics: from nature and wildlife to Russian history and religion, to his love life, political views, and philosophy on life. He even wrote poems about his imaginary 'enemies'[6]. But whatever the subject matter, no reader is ever left untouched.

Even writing this now I feel tempted to put an 'equal to' sign between Esenin's name and his poems - only that would be too easy; nor would it do him justice. All that depth of feeling - desire, wisdom, shame, and sorrow - contained in his verses, would have seemed too much for one person to have experienced in their lifetime (and Esenin's life was quite short – only thirty years). Yet there it was, so how did he do it?

Weirdly, I think of Esenin's poetic gift more as the fifth element, a radio set fine-tuned to receive, decode and broadcast messages from the Macrocosm. This must have been how he got most of his poetic inspiration. And who knows – following some perverse

---

6 Poem ' The Dark Man', 197

logic - maybe the things he wrote about did play a role in determining the course of his life?

***

Like his work, Esenin himself was full of controversies. His reputation as a habitual drunkard and fearless ruffian goes hand in hand with the accolades for his literature. Younger Russians seem to respect that most in him. To them, Esenin is like a best mate, a bookish hardcase, whose wild side is excused by flashes of poetic genius and whose perfect imperfection and at-full-blast lifestyle is something to aspire to. The best testament to that juvenile bromance could be a catchphrase that is very popular on Russian social networking websites today. It goes like this: 'Если ты пьёшь, как Есенин, то где твои стихи?' ('If you drink like Esenin, where are your poems?')

When I was at secondary school (in the era of beeping pagers and telephones with cords), Esenin was everyone's favourite in our Russian Literature class. No other poet ever solicited even one affectionate diminutive nickname from my classmates as far as I can recall. Sergei Esenin had a few: Seryozha (Russian for 'little Sergei'), Seriy, and Sergunek.

Decades later, I was pleasantly surprised to learn from my niece, who was finishing secondary school the year I started work on the book, that it was the same for her Russian literature class, too. And it is this intergenerational continuity of emotional allegiance to the poet that makes him so 'Russian' in my eyes.

***

Sergei Esenin may have thought that it was Pushkin, the unrivalled storyteller and prophet, who laid the foundations of Russian language and culture, giving shape to everything we now call 'the Russian way'. To some degree, Esenin may have even dreamed of repeating Pushkin's literary destiny. Yet it would soon prove to be more that of Mikhail Lermontov's[7] – fast and tragic, almost a fantasy.

---

[7] Mikhail Yurievich Lermontov (1814-1841) – Russian romantic poet and writer, founder of the Russian psychological novel. He often seemed engulfed with strong passions, blues and fatalistic moods. One might even say that Lermontov died through folly. He allegedly teased former Cadet school friend Nikolai Martynov over his resemblance to Grushnitsky, main

18

'Did I live at all or did I dream?' *

Esenin was to become merely a character, another chapter in the book of his own life. That book, however, was defined by the conventions of Esenin's own artistic genre: if Lermontov's life looked more like a romantic ballad, Esenin's was more of a folktale, albeit with a downbeat ending.

This was how Boris Pasternak, the internationally acclaimed author of *'Doktor Zhivago'* and 1958 Noble Prize winner for Literature, saw Esenin's fate, of which he gave the following interpretation: 'Esenin lived in a sort of fairy tale. He flew across the sea Ivan-Tsarevich style and caught Isadora Duncan in her toils as if she were the Firebird.[9] His poetry was nothing short of fantastic ingenuity, too: now he played a game of Patience with words, now used his own blood for ink.[10]

---

character of Lermontov's successful novel *'A Hero of Our Time'*; so Martynov challenged Lermontov to a duel and shot him to death. (Wikipedia)

[8] Poem 'No regrets, no entreating, no crying...' , 129

[9] Ivan-Tsarevich and the Firebird are characters from the Russian folktale 'Ivan-Tsarevich, the Firebird, and the Grey Wolf'. Catching the elusive Firebird (a symbol of wisdom and prosperity) and bringing it home to his tsar father was Ivan Tsarevich's mission and the plot's central twist.

[10] Poem 'Goodbye, my friend, it's time to leave' (211), allegedly written in own blood a day before or on the day he died.

The gem of his poetic style is the image of his native landscape: woody, Eastern European, Ryazan[11], conveyed with mind-blowing freshness – just the way he had seen it as a child.' (Collected prose "People and Situations", 1956)*

Today, in the age of social lifts and equal opportunities, it would surprise no one if an ambitious young person from the country made a successful career in the capital. But in early twentieth-century Russia, a 'peasant boy' making a name for himself as a notable poet was nothing short of a fairy tale. Esenin's rise to fame was unprecedented.

Let's now take a look at how and why Esenin's folktale was born.

---

[11] Ryazan - in nineteenth-century Russian Empire, a province where Esenin hailed from; today, the administrative centre of Ryazan Oblast.

EARLY YEARS AND GLORY

Sergei Aleksandrovich[12] Esenin was born on October 3, 1895, in Konstantinovo village in what is today Ryazan Oblast, one hundred and ninety-six kilometres southeast of Moscow, on the Oka River. His parents, well-to-do farmers Alexander and Tatiana Esenin, didn't get on very well, as theirs was an arranged marriage. Shortly after Sergei's birth, Tatiana moved out to live with her parents, and from about the age of two, the boy was in the full custody of his loving grandparents and three maternal uncles. The granddad, Nikita Titov, was a great fan of church literature, and the granny was an expert in Slavic folk songs, fairy tales, and couplets; something which would later have an immense influence on Esenin's early style.

---

[12] Aleksandrovich is what's called a 'patronymic', which is an integral part of one's full name in some Eastern European cultures.

Esenin learnt to read at around the age of five; a few years later he attempted his very first verses. *"I began to versify early on. Granny was the catalyst. She would tell me folktales. I didn't like some of the ones with bad endings, so I would rewrite them in my mind. My first poems were modelled on folk couplets."**

Esenin's teenage friend Nikolai Sardanovskiy later reminisced in his memoirs that he had been among the first to experience the magic of Esenin's verse. It was 1910, and Esenin had already written quite a few; his early poems were all largely depictive and lyrical.

In 1912, aged seventeen and fresh out of secondary school, Esenin moved to Moscow and got a job as a proof-reader's assistant at a printing shop: a perfect occupation for the bibliophile that he was, as it provided access to scores of books and important contacts from the world of publishing. During that time he became a member of the then-popular Surikov Literary and Musical Circle, a literary association of self-taught writers from among the common people. Esenin's first partner, Anna Izryadnova, described the

Esenin of that period as an avid and liberal reader: "He was known to be forward-minded, an active distributor of the clandestine press. He would spend all his spare time and money on books and periodicals, with little consideration to day-to-day living, or his future..."*

In 1913 Esenin enrolled into the historical and philosophical faculty of the People's University of Shanyavsky, Russia's first free Open University, where he heard a course of lectures on Western European Literature, and on Russian poets. A year later, however, Esenin quit both his job and university to immerse himself in poetry. In January 1914, he had his debut poem – 'The Birch Tree' – published in a children's magazine 'Mirok' (Little World).

***

As is almost always the case with creative individuals, Esenin's success was to be based on the 'Muhammad must come to the mountain' scenario. In 1915, aged eighteen, he began to wonder why he had not received the recognition he thought he deserved - and set off for

Petrograd[13]. The first poet on his 'to visit' list was Alexander Blok[14], who left the following entry concerning the visit in his diary: 'A peasant of Ryazan province, aged 19. Fresh, crisp, fluent, vociferous writing'.

Blok immediately introduced Esenin to the then fashionable poet Sergey Gorodetsky who had been throwing parties for Petrograd's poetic elite. Esenin's folktale took off.

Gorodetsky, in turn, introduced Esenin to poet Nikolai Kluev, whose predominantly epic style, inspired by the folklore of the Russian North, would have a profound and long-term influence on Esenin's work.

Esenin's debut book 'Radunitsa'[15], comprising fifteen poems, came out in 1916 and was well-received. Naïve and sweet, the poems focused on nature, Russian Orthodox church holidays, rural agriculture, and the

---

[13] The name given to St Petersburg by the Imperial government at the outbreak of WWI, in order to expunge the German reference (burg) (Wikipedia)

[14] Aleksander Aleksandrovich Blok (1880-1921) – Russian lyrical poet of the Silver Age.

[15] Radunitsa – in Russian Orthodox tradition, a church fete of the Universal Commemoration of the Departed (usually comes after Easter).

seasons.

In a preface to one of the reprints of the book, Esenin wrote: *"Some stages in my career need clarifying, the most controversial one being my early days' religiousness. The literary scene of 1913-14-15 had the same mood and mindset as that of my grandparents', and so my poems were savoured with the relish that now makes me cringe. I am neither a church member nor a mystic. I am a realist and romanticist. But my romanticism is rather down-to-earth. I kindly ask my readers to treat the notions of Jesus, Godmother, and Mykolas[16] in my early poems simply as folktale characters. I cannot disown that phase in my poetic career by simply crossing it out, just like mankind cannot cross out the two thousand years of Christian culture. The backbone of my poems is lyrical sentiment, and imagery - for the latter constitutes the essence of the Russian mind and soul"**.

This distinct 'peasant' simplicity was indeed the hallmark of all Esenin's early work. Yet some verses about wildlife were charged with painstaking detail and brutal realism. The poems 'The Cow', 'The Vixen', and 'Ode to the Dog', although traditionally regarded as written for the younger audience, are a laborious read

---

[16]Mykola – old Russian church name for St. Nicholas.

and may even reduce one to tears. They certainly affected the literary superstar Maxim Gorky[17], who wrote the following about his experience of Esenin's poems:

"The impression produced by Esenin's reading was quite overpowering. It was painful to listen to him, painful to tears. …It was impossible to believe that such a little man could possess such enormous power of feeling, such perfect expressiveness… He thrilled me so much that a lump rose to my throat and I felt like sobbing. <> I told him that, in my opinion, he was the first poet in Russian literature to write about animals with such sincere love and with such skill. <> I asked him if he knew Paul Claudel's 'Paradise of Animals'. He did not reply, felt his head with both hands, and began to read 'The Song of a Dog'. When he uttered the last lines – 'The dog's eyes rolled like golden stars onto the snow' – his eyes too filled with tears."

***

---

[17] Maxim Gorky (born Alexei Maximovich Peshkov) (1868-1936) – Russian and Soviet writer and political activist, founder of the socialist realism literary method. He had a close association with fellow Russian writers Leo Tolstoy and Anton Chekhov and would later mention them in his memoirs. (Wikipedia)

Some of Esenin's early work was so intensely figurative that Russian language scholars would decades later theorise that it contained a coded narration of the ideology of ancient pagan Slavs. One such example is this four-liner:

> *Yonder, amid cabbage patches,*
> *Watered by light from the red rising dawn,*
> *A small maple tree has found refuge*
> *And feeds on the green teat of Earth.**

It is common knowledge today that ancient Slavs were pagan. Slavic paganism, as a system of traditions, rituals, and beliefs, is still so deeply rooted in the Russian mind that it may be impossible to say where it ends and where Russian Orthodox faith begins. Indeed, most Russian Orthodox believers, although realising that superstition is frowned upon by the Church, will commonly spit over their left shoulder to ward off evil, or avoid looking in the mirror if they need to pop back in for something immediately after leaving home (as it is considered a bad omen; in Slavic culture, mirrors were always considered the gates to the netherworld).

One could speculate long and hard about the phenomenon of Slavic paganism, its uniqueness and complexity. What is relevant to the story, however, are the two aspects of it, namely polytheism and a reverence for nature. The latter seems the key to understanding the four-liner, as the sun was the pinnacle deity in the ancient Slavic mythology, the reason for all existence. Hence, scholars argued that Esenin's metaphoric referral to the light of dawn acting as water was supposed to tell us just that. The use of the words 'water' and 'red' in describing dawn somehow brings up the image of blood, thus consolidating the allusion to the Sun as a living thing: the light of Dawn, or the blood of the Sun, giving life to everything on Earth.

Another symbolic reference here is the maple tree feeding on the green teat of Earth. Following the first example, this might be an allusion to the affinity of humanity and Nature, whereby humanity can only survive as long as Mother Nature does - a fundamental concept that is the anthem of the environmentalism movement. Unbeknown to him, Esenin had brought this up long before environmental damage became an issue in the twentieth century.

Equally, in another poem ("Ancient world, my mysterious world…", 121) he likened motorways to stone hands squashing the countryside's neck.

Esenin saw the imminent urbanisation of the Empire as a tragedy for Russian village life and, in a way, for the Russian mentality nurtured on centuries of pagan Slavic wisdom. He could almost sense the inevitable and irrevocable loss of everything that had represented the Russian world to him: morality and inner harmony. The conflict between the country and the big city, wilderness and civilisation, was a recurring theme.

This conflict was also something of a personal affair for Esenin who was a countryman through and through, and who came to miss his village past dearly while living in the 'wider world'. The wrenching nostalgia for the simplicity of his rustic ways was one of Esenin's main poetic messages. In the bestselling and époque-defining novel 'Up in the Air' by Walter Kirn, I came across a sentence which seems to summarise perfectly this truly universal conflict phenomenon: "...the migration from the village to the city, the disillusionment with urban wickedness, and the mournful desire to go home."[18]

In his divinatory, poetic way Esenin also heralded the dawn of what would later develop into a 'gluten-free' concept by modern nutritional scientists. In the poem 'Song of the Bread', he juxtaposed the simple pleasure of eating freshly baked bread with the process of making it, grimly likening the latter to the torture and desecration of a living being.

Again, Esenin's Slavic collective unconscious treated wheat as a living and breathing thing. Moreover, in these two four-lines, he stated an uncanny truth about the alleged effects of gluten on human bodies:

> *Once the poor dough has been fermented,*
> *They will bake a lot of tasty treats...*
> *This is when the whitish poison enters*
> *Our guts - to lay its eggs of spleen.*

---

[18] Kirn, Walter. Up in the Air. John Murray (Publishers); 2010, 9.

Passing off all beatings, pain and rudeness
For the bread's delicious golden crust,
This white killer acts the same as dead meat,
*Poisoning and spoiling people's guts.**

It is no wonder that, according to the poet's childhood pal Nikolai Sardanovskiy, Esenin had at some point in his life been vegetarian.

***

In January 1916, with WWI in full swing, Esenin was called up for military service. In the spring, however, the young poet and some of his friends were invited to recite in front of the Great Empress Alexandra Fyodorovna, wife of Nicholas II. This fateful event may have helped him escape a trip to the front line.

***

A year later, in the spring of 1917, Esenin frequented the editorial office of the 'People's Cause' newspaper where he met one Zinaida Reich. They married in July of that year. The tumult of the Great Revolution (that would climax in October) had picked up the pace, providing a dramatic backdrop to their love story.

If anything, there was a certain similarity in how they both died. Having outlived Esenin by fourteen years, Reich was brutally murdered in her own flat in 1939, only months after her second husband (theatre director Vsevolod Meyerhold) was arrested and subsequently executed by the NKVD[19].

***

Esenin embraced the Great October Revolution fully and unconditionally, mainly because of what it had promised to do for the peasantry. He believed in land redistribution, the Bolsheviks' commitment to rural literacy and education, and the general euphoria of regeneration. And the new regime seemed to love him back. The term 'people's poet' that I mentioned previously and that had become characteristic of Esenin's persona, had been attributed to him during his lifetime. Call it the Russian naivety, or the silly optimism

---

[19] NKVD stood for NarKomat Vnutrennih Del (People's Committee for Home Affairs) and represented a sinister governmental body dealing with everything from policing and censorship to national security. (Wikipedia)

of youth, but Esenin welcomed the Revolution to become one of its heralds. Only his support was short-lived. And as the gruesome reality of the civil war and famine shook the former Empire, he grew more and more disillusioned.

Naturally, there was a price tag attached to everything to do with Bolshevik rule, and Esenin was soon to find that out. His very life would be the price for denouncing the new regime.

***

Pre-empting myself, the matter of Esenin's death had been some sort of national mystery throughout the twentieth century - mainly because everything concerning Esenin's case had been under wraps until the collapse of the Soviet Union, when former state archives were opened to the public.

In 2005 a TV drama 'Esenin' starring, among the best Russian actors, the American Sean Young as Isadora Duncan, offered a fictionalised investigation by a real detective who got his hands on the archives to reveal some unexpected evidence. By 'real detective', I mean that the person portrayed in the TV series – Eduard Khlystalov - was a real life person and a former senior official at the MVD (Ministry for Home Affairs) of the USSR; he wrote a few books on Esenin's alleged murder in the '90s. I will come back to that point later to cast doubt on Esenin's 'suicide' that to this day haunts his name, dominating nearly every online article about the poet that you can find in the English language.

***

Halfway through his career (1918-1921), Esenin published his second book of poems - 'Goluben' [20] - and co-founded a poetic flow, Imaginism, inside the Russian avant-garde, which came after the Revolution of 1917. Imaginists created poetry based on sequences of arresting and uncommon images. They used metaphors widely, sometimes producing long chains of them in their poems, to create a sense of dynamism and verblessness (Wikipedia). This temporary enchantment

---

[20] Goluben (old Russian) - a poetic reference to the Cambridge blue of the skies.

with the power of imagery resulted in two more books of poems published in 1921: 'Treryadnitsa'[21] and 'Confession of a Hooligan'.

Being somewhat experimental, the Imaginist movement soon rendered itself irrelevant, thus reinstating the supremacy of 'organic', gimmick-free poetry. The same year Esenin went travelling around Eastern Russia, visiting the Urals and Central Asia.

***

In 1922 Esenin met and subsequently married the free-spirited American dancing sensation, Isadora Duncan. This rather brief love story was truly romantic, given that neither spoke more than three words of each other's language. Esenin accompanied Isadora on her tour of Europe and America, and by the time they returned to Soviet Russia (1923), the marriage had effectively broken up.

A lot of books were written on both Isadora and her Russian adventures (including her own

---

[21] Treryadnitsa – a Russian orthodox old-rite icon comprising three rows or tiers filled with holly images.

autobiography 'My Life'), all of them providing unique and truly insightful accounts of her relationship with the poet.

And yes, women were wild about Esenin. He certainly had a way of making them fall for him. It didn't seem to take much to encourage them. He was just himself and smiled, and along they would come. With three marriages and numerous romantic involvements under his belt, he had made relationships look like child's play. He parted with women just as easily, too. But none seemed to have ever become his enemy: they must all have felt somewhat blessed to have been his muses and to have had him in their lives, even for a short time.

To be fair to Esenin, although fully aware of the effect his appearance had on women (with his cornflower blue eyes and the mane of golden, slightly curly hair), he was in no way a narcissist. While obviously taking pride in his appearance and naturally wanting to uphold the newly acquired image of the next big thing in Russian poetry, Esenin had never made it his main 'weapon' – he didn't need to. Everyone, men and women, felt equally drawn to the powerful poetic gift of his. This is best illustrated in an excerpt from the memoirs by Isadora's Soviet impresario, Ilya Ilyitch Schneider.

In his book 'Isadora Duncan: The Russian Years', Schneider offered the following recollection of Esenin and Duncan's first encounter.

"Yakulov's studio[22] was on the top floor of a tall house, somewhere in Sadovaya street. The appearance of Duncan, that evening, produced an immediate hush, followed by an inconceivable hubbub in which the name of Duncan could be heard again and again. Yakulov beamed with pleasure.

Suddenly I was nearly knocked down by a man in a light grey coat. He kept turning his head this way and that and shouting: 'Where's Duncan? Where's Duncan?'

'Who's that?', I asked Yakulov.

'Esenin', he answered, laughing.

I had seen Esenin a few times, but only in passing, and I had not recognised him just now.

---

[22] Georgiy Yakulov (1884-1928) – Soviet avant-garde artist best known for designing the memorial to the Twenty-six Baku Comissars.

A little later, Yakulov and I went up to Isadora. She was reclining on a sofa. Esenin was kneeling beside her and she was stroking his hair, scanning: -Za-la-ta-ya ga-la-va' (golden head).

There was such ease between the two that evening that it was impossible to believe they had just met. They seemed to have known each other a long time.[23]

Yakulov introduced me. I looked attentively at Esenin. In spite of the Russian proverb "Ill-fame runs and good fame lies down", he seemed to be haunted by both sorts of fame at one and the same time: the fame of his poems in which there was genuine poetry, and the fame of his brawls and eccentric behaviour.

He was rather short and, for all his elegance, a little stout. His eyes were unforgettable: blue with an almost embarrassed look. There was nothing harsh about him, neither in his features nor in the expression of his eyes.

Without rising from his knees, Esenin turned to us and said: "I was told Duncan was at the Hermitage. I rushed off there…"

Isadora again buried her hand in 'the gold of his hair'… that was how, afterwards, they 'talked' with each other all through the night, apparently with full

---

[23] The excerpt comes from the English translation of Schneider's original book, written in Russian and titled 'Vstrechi s Eseninym' (Encounters with Esenin). For some reason, parts of the original text were omitted in the translation. For this particular description, I translated and re-introduced the missing bits in bold, as they are important for the narration.

understanding.

'He read me his poems', Isadora told me later that night. 'I couldn't understand a thing but there was music in them, they could have only been written by a genie" (genie – French for 'genius').

To further illustrate Esenin's hectic nature and eccentricity, I would like to quote here another account of the same event - this time by poet Anatoly Mariengoff, as recollected by Irma Duncan (arguably Isadora's favourite disciple) in her book 'Isadora Duncan's Russian Days and her Last Years in France'[24]:

In a novel recently written by Mariengoff and titled: *"A Novel Without Lies"*, there is set down the story of the days passed together by the two poets. In one part of his story, the narrator tells of an evening they spent in the Ermitage, a sort of summer amusement park in Moscow. The well-known futurist artist and stage decorator for the Kamerny Theatre, George Jacouloff, came towards them and without any prelude said:

"Do you want me to introduce you to Isadora Duncan?"

[24] Irma Duncan, Alan Ross Mcdougall. Isadora Duncan's Russian Days and her Last Years in France. Victor Gollancz Ltd; 1929, 97-100.

Essenine[25] jumped from his seat.

"Where is she? Where!"

"Here. She's a wonderful woman."

Essenine seized Jacouloff by the hand: "Take us to her right away!"

We started off looking for Isadora. From the Mirrored Room to the Winter Theatre; from the Winter Theatre to the Summer Theatre; from the Summer Theatre to the Operette; and from there back again to the Park, looking at all the benches. But there was no sign anywhere of Isadora Duncan.

"Devil take it! She must have left."

"Here, George, here!"

And again we ran to the Mirrored Room, to the Winter Theatre and from the Winter Theatre to the Operette, to the Summer Theatre, to the Park.

"George, dear, here, here!"

I said: "What's the matter, Sergei? What's biting you?"

Essenine was sombre and annoyed. Now it seems

---

[25] Throughout her book, Irma spelt all Russian proper names the French way, which seems only natural, given the amount of time she had spent with Isadora in France.

that there was something fatal in his feverish, inexplicable desire to meet this woman he had never seen, and who was to play in his life a role so great, so sad. I might even say pernicious. At the same time I hasten to add that the influence that Isadora Duncan had over Essenine does not in any way lower this wonderful woman, this great human being, this artist of genius."

'Some time later Isadora went to tea at Jacouloff's studio. There were many artists and poets gathered there, but Essenine was not among them. The host was disappointed that he had not turned up before the dancer left. He made arrangements to have an evening party the following week and asked Isadora if she would care to come again. She was in her element with the Bohemian company and was only too pleased to accept the invitation. Besides, such gay[26] parties were few and far between in that epoch. Isadora, therefore, on the evening of the party, decked herself out in her favourite red dress, arranged her hair and perfumed herself as though she was on the way to supper at the house of her friend Cecile Sorel in Paris. She arrived at the Jacouloff studio after midnight. Mariengoff, who was there, describes her entrance and what followed:

"...She advanced slowly, with grace. She looked round the room with eyes that seemed like saucers of blue delft, and her gaze was stopped by the sight of Essenine. Her mouth, small and delicate, smiled at him. Isadora then reclined on the couch, and Essenine came

---

[26] 'Gay' here is used in its original meaning of 'merry', 'fun'. Not to be confused with the contemporary, secondary meaning.

and sat at her feet. She ran her fingers through his curly hair and said: 'Solotaya golova!' (Golden head!)' We were surprised to hear her say these two words, she who only knew about a dozen Russian words all told. Then she kissed him on the lips, and again from her mouth, small and red like a bullet-wound, came with pleasant caressing accent, a Russian word: 'Anguel!' (Angel!), she kissed him again and said: 'Tchort!' (Devil!)

At four o'clock in the morning Isadora Duncan and Essenine left…"

It is curious how different in nuance and style these two accounts are, yet both paint a vivid and authentic picture of that fateful encounter. And somewhere in the overlapping area, no doubt lays a well-balanced truth.

***

But the picture of this love story would not be complete without yet another excerpt from Irma's book which, to me, perfectly sums up Esenin's wild side, while also representing a lot of the boisterous, straight-talking Russian spirit so often frowned upon in the West:

"A few evenings later, Isadora was entertaining some friends in her studio. In the dimly lighted room, whose blue draperies seemed to reach far up into space, there was a calm, an almost religious silence, for Isadora had just danced a Chopin mazurka. The onlookers had seen before their eyes one lovely movement melting into another – beauty made manifest. And as the last notes of the piano died away, and Isadora walked towards her silent, moved friends, whose clouded eyes spoke their thanks, the exalted mood of the moment was shattered by a dozen feet pounding on the stairs and half a dozen drunken voices lifted in raucous laughter and vinous wit.

Into the room – the calm Isadoran temple – there burst a group of Imaginist poets led by Essenine and Kousikoff with his omnipresent balalaika. The high priestess, who at any other time would have driven the intruders forth with words more cutting than whip-thongs, welcomed there noisy followers of Bacchus and Apollo.

Through a friendly interpreter, she said to Essenine, whom she was overjoyed to see: 'I'm going to do a dance all for you!' She arose from her divan and asked the pianist to play a Chopin waltz that she felt would appeal to the lyric soul of the golden-haired poet. And with what rapturous joy and seductive grace she moved through the rhythms of the dance! When the music ended she came forward with her ingenuous smile, her eyes radiant, her hands outstretched towards Essenine, who was now talking loudly to his companions, and she asked him how he had liked her dance. The interpreter translated. Essenine said something coarse and brutal that brought howls of coarse and brutal laughter from his drunken friends. The friend who was acting as interpreter said with evident hesitation to Isadora: 'He says it was – awful… and that he can do better than that himself!'

And even before the whole speech was translated to the crestfallen and humiliated Isadora, the poet was on his feet dancing about the studio like a crazy man. The balalaika twanged, and his fellow Bohemians shouted approvingly.

Music, peace, grace, beauty – all had flown from the temple as the roisterers had tramped in, and they were soon followed by the friends, who, earlier in the evening, had received their benediction."

The latter example may not speak in Esenin's favour. Moreover, one may feel rather sorry for Isadora, whose dancing had been so rudely ridiculed. Running ahead, a similar thing would later happen to Esenin in America, when he would be mocked for 'spilling his heart' in front of the bourgeois crowd. Call it life's funny way of giving one's due, or else – a lesson against casting pearls… But what genius is ever fully understood and accepted when they need it most? Neither of them were lacking in genius; only Duncan received more praise than criticism in her lifetime.

I could go on and on, telling you about Esenin's early days and his poetic style. But the truth is — his life is in his verse, so the best way to get acquainted with and to understand Sergei Esenin is simply to read his poems.

LATER YEARS AND DEATH

Esenin's marriage to Isadora Duncan came to an end in 1923, shortly after the pair returned to Soviet Russia from Isadora's tour of Europe and the USA. Visiting New York and rural America gave Esenin much food for thought. He reconsidered many aspects of life back home, as well as his attitude towards the Communist cause.

These new ideas and moods of a somewhat refreshed and changed Esenin resulted in a short essay *'Iron Mirgorod[27]'* and are best summed up in this episode on the liner 'Paris' that had carried Esenin across the Atlantic:

'I had just entered the ship's restaurant, which was a little bigger than the Bolshoi Theatre, when our travel companion

---

[27] An allusion to the collection of short stories by iconic nineteenth-century Russian writer Nikolai Gogol; Gogol's 'Mirgorod' was a satirical portrayal of provincial Russian/Ukrainian life.

approached me to say that I was expected in our cabin.

I made my way back through gigantic halls, libraries, recreation rooms, where people played cards, the dance hall, and some five minutes later finally reached the hall leading to our cabin. I examined the ante-room full of our luggage (nearly twenty suitcases), the dining area, my room, and the two ensuites. Then I sat down on the sofa and broke into loud laughter. The world I had lived in before seemed to me at once terribly comic and absurd.

I remembered my homeland, my village, where almost every muzhik[28] keeps his pigs or calves in the house; and after the German and Belgian motorways, our Russian roads seemed to me ever heavier. I cursed everyone clinging to Ancient Rus as if it were a synonym for dirt and lousiness. This was when I stopped loving the poverty-ridden Russia.

My dear sirs!

That was also when I became an ardent supporter of the Communist cause. I may not be at one with the communists in my poems, or in my heart - but I can relate to them intellectually. And, hopefully, this will be reflected in my work.'*

My original plan was to translate 'Iron Mirgorod' in

---

[28] Muzhik - boor, Russian peasant.

full, but I reconsidered this for two main reasons. Firstly, although being rather short, the essay has an extensive list of endnotes providing nearly the same amount of text, if not more – and I don't know anyone who is excited about reading endnotes. Secondly, Esenin's overall impression of America was still far from flattering; some of the terms he used to describe its urban and rural population and their ways are rather arguable and might not be deemed politically correct in the current socio-political climate (although what is considered a no-no today was quite alright to say in Esenin's time).

But just to give the readers an example, Esenin wrote a letter to his friend, Alexander Sakharov, saying: *"What can I tell you about this awful kingdom of bourgeoisie that borders on idiocy? There is nothing here, except the foxtrot. Gobbling, drinking and again foxtrotting. I haven't yet met a real human here and don't know where to search for him. Mister dollar is terribly fashionable, and they don't give a damn about art - the most sophisticated thing for them is the music hall."*

He made a series of similar observations which,

when considered collectively and from the perspective of different mentalities, make *'Iron Mirgorod'* a guide to understanding the eternal, irreconcilable differences between Russian and Western ways.

On a positive note, America did impress Esenin more than Europe, and he concluded the essay with this, *'Europe smokes and tosses out the stubs. America picks them up and turns into something extraordinary.'*

***

To cut a long story short, the America-Europe tour was an unfortunate enterprise for Duncan and Esenin. Tarnished with a series of provocations which triggered scandalous behaviour by both of them, and accusations of spreading Bolshevist propaganda, they were first invited to leave America and later, made to leave France in a hurry, amidst the French government's threats to commit Esenin to a public lunatic asylum.

In reply to multiple newspaper attacks, Isadora published an open letter in the French *Nouvelle Revue* and the New York *Herald*, saying: "I took Esenin away from Russia where the conditions of life are still very difficult. I wanted to save him for the world. Now he is returning to Russia to save his reason, for he cannot live without Russia. I know that many hearts will offer up prayers for this great poet so that he may live to create beauty in future."

And return back home to his beloved Russia he did.

***

Esenin's newly found Bolshevik enthusiasm, however, soon began to wear off, as the aftermath of the October Revolution and the resulting Civil War had turned more and more sinister. News of unrest kept coming in from around the former Empire: the peasant riot in Tambov province, the Kronstadt rebellion (a major unsuccessful uprising of the Navy against the Bolsheviks in March 1921); hunger was rife too. Esenin was outraged, and that was naturally reflected in his poems. For it pained him to realise that his nation had so abruptly lost what it had stood for since the dawn of civilisation: the sense of conscience and justice, kindness, love, and faith (both human and religious).

The year 1923 also saw another of his books published – *'Hooligan's poems'*, followed by *'Tavern Moscow'* and a narrative poem *'Pugachev'* (1924); and later - the cycle of romantic poems *'Persian Motifs'*, inspired by his 1925 travels in the Caucasus.

Both books, the *'Hooligan's poems'* and *'Tavern Moscow'*, cemented the image of Esenin which is most commonly known to the Russian masses – that of a brawler, drunkard, womaniser, and an expert user of Russian swear words – or 'mat' [mʌt], as they call it over there. The poems of that period were raucous, unromantic, full of expletives and self-deprecation, and rather cynical. But so was the new world around him. To Esenin, a fervent fan of his native tongue, *mat* was not just a means of expressing disappointment or anger; it was a mode of communication with others – and quite an effective one, too. This vital social function of *mat*, by the way, remains popular in Russian culture to this day.

Here, as before, the recollections by Ilya Schneider

are most valuable in terms of illustrating my point. In the excerpt below, Schneider reminisces about a funny conversation he had with Isadora Duncan on their way back from a party:

'I remember driving much later in a cab with Isadora. She could not stand slow driving and she asked me to tell the cabman to drive faster, which I did. The cabman jerked the reins, smacked his lips, uttered his famous 'gee-up', and soon relapsed into his former languid state. Isadora asked me again to hurry him up. I did so with the same result.

"You're not telling him properly," Isadora cried angrily. "Now, Esenin always says something which makes them drive fast at once."

'I tried all the traditional ways of urging cabbies to speed up, but it was no good.

"No, no," explained Isadora, "those are not the words he used. Esenin says something very short and very strong, just as in a game of chess. I can't remember it. But whatever it is it makes them drive off at a spanking pace."

'I did not care to repeat Esenin's vocabulary in Isadora's presence.'

***

Back to Esenin's later work, though. In a history poem *'Pugachev'*, he drew direct and unflattering parallels between the eighteenth-century uprising against Empress Catherine II, led by Don Cossack Emelyan Pugachev, and the state of things in the country after the revolution and civil war. According to Russian history textbooks, Pugachev was not only the rebel leader, but the impostor and pretender to the Russian throne. Russian literary scholars' unanimous stance on this poetic narration is that Esenin really wanted to denounce the Bolsheviks who, unlike Pugachev, did manage to seize power, plunging the country into complete chaos.

In one of his last iconic pieces, the narrative poem *'Land of Scoundrels'*, written in 1922-23, Esenin went as far as to explicitly attack Soviet Russian leaders for their alleged Russophobic views and attitudes - a move that brought scathing criticism and a ban on his work. Apparently, some leaders saw a great deal of themselves in the poem's main characters; and everything those characters said must have hit the spot, making it even easier to recognise the prototypes. Unsurprisingly,

Esenin became an ideological threat overnight.

One of the poem's central figures, commissioner Chekistov[29], is traditionally considered a literary personification of Leon Trotsky, a Communist ideologist and Party activist, who in his early days held the title of People's Commissar for Foreign Affairs.

Throughout the poem, which is an eclectic mix of rhyming and prose (more akin in style to a theatrical play), Esenin's Chekistov dished out anti-Russian rhetoric charged with loathing for the 'muzhiks of the Russian plains':

Zamarashkin[30]: «Easy on abuse, Chekistov!
Your swearing makes even this signal booth turn red.

<...>

This [spoiled, scanty food] *is really nothing, brother -*

---

[29] Like most surnames in the poem, 'Chekistov' is a charactonym (a literary technique used to make characters' names speak for themselves, revealing their true core). Thus 'Checkistov' screams 'chekist', which was the nickname for the agents of Cheka, the first of a succession of Soviet secret police organizations, whose short name in Russian read: "Чрезвычайная Коммиссия", or ЧК [che-ka] (Wikipedia). Cheka had evolved a lot during the Soviet era and has been also known as OGPU, NKVD, and most recently KGB and MVD.

[30] 'Zamarashkin' is also a charactonym and stems from the Russian verb 'zamaratj' ('to soil', 'to profane').

Some people have to eat each other.
There… Near Samara … I heard…
What a nasty year we've had!

Chekistov: «*Look at your own people, the lazy brood,*
They wouldn't help themselves, even if they could.
Nothing is as dull and double-faced
As your muzhiks of the Russian plains!
…What a difference Europe makes.

<…>

I curse and am willing to damn you
For another one thousand years -
I just want to go to a restroom,
But you have none in this place.
You're a weird and funny folk –
Have lived poverty-stricken for ages,
Yet built your enormous churches…
If it were down to me,
I'd have turned them all into bench-holes.*

On a separate note, *'Land of Scoundrels'* also targeted materialism and capitalism in their most demoralising (according to Esenin) form – the vulgarisation of society:

Rain of stock and shower of shares
Pelt on top hats, derbies, and caps.
There you have the wider world's shackles,
There you have global swindlers and cheats.
If one wanted to spill one's heart there,
They would say: he's stupid or sloshed.
There you have the global stock market!
*There you have all the scums of this world!**

The above fragment describes Esenin's feelings about America's business community and its practices. Incidentally, the United States was mentioned a lot in the poem, and certain parallels were drawn between the American and Bolshevik ways. This may have been because the work on the poem had begun during Esenin and Duncan's tour of Europe and America, so it would only have been natural for him to draw on those fresh experiences in creating the poem's central conflict.

While there were a lot of things he admired in America, having experienced or seen them for the first time, the general impression of American bourgeois society left Esenin depressed. Not so much because no one there seemed to recognise him as Soviet Russia's star poet, but because he simply didn't fit in mentality-wise. So much so, he would always sing the Soviet anthem 'The Internationale' at the high-profile parties that Isadora attended, embarrassing both himself and his wife – simply as a protest. Those notorious tantrums would always end in disaster. But soon enough, the initial shock and dislike for the dancer's eccentric Russian husband turned into a mockery and became a form of entertainment for the New York high-life. And the more they mocked Esenin, the more he 'protested' – the kind of weird emotional masochism that is often attributed to my compatriots.

That said, it is important to remember that *'Land of Scoundrels'* was not about America, but rather about the new, post-Revolutionary land of the Soviets.

***

Shortly after his return to Russia, Esenin was introduced to the poet and translator Wolf Erlich, 23, who was to become his softly-spoken friend and something of an ecstatic disciple. Erlich would literally shadow Esenin everywhere, and he was the last person to see Esenin alive on the night he died at St Petersburg's historic five-star Hotel Angleterre.

It seems rather indicative that in 1925, the year Esenin died, Erlich was employed as an attendant at the adjacent Astoria hotel[31], then known as Pervyi Dom Leningradskogo Soveta (First House of the Leningrad Soviet) and rumoured to have close links with Chekists. This fact seems to validate some scholarly opinion that Erlich had been a Chekist informer appointed to watch the patriotic, reactionary poet.

***

Meanwhile, Esenin's civil verse turned even more bitter and bolder. One poem in particular *("Снова пьют здесь, дерутся и плачут…" / "Endless drinking, and fighting, and sobbing…", 1922)** seemed to have been so controversial that numerous edits had to be made, resulting in two equally popular versions available today – the official (print one) and the unofficial (allegedly used by Esenin

---

[31] In the 1920-30s, both Angleterre and Astoria were neighbouring sister hotels. In the 1970s, for some time, Angleterre had become part of the Astoria complex only to be split off later after a series of renovations. Today's Hotel Angleterre is marketed as the business-class wing of its more luxurious sister.

during public poetry recitals, as recorded in the memoirs of his ex-partner and life-long admirer Galina Benislavskaya).

Endless drinking, and fighting, and sobbing
To accordion's yellow blues.
People damning their fate and misfortunes,
Looking back on Muscovian Rus.

<...>

There is something we've lost so awfully.
Oh, my blue May, my pale blue June!
Must be why everything reeks of offal,
Rooted up by this hopeless carouse...

The following two four-liners, however, never made it into censored print at the time:

Oh, protect me, the mellowy dampness,
Dark blue May and pale blue June!
We've been ridden by hostile strangers
Treating us, the insiders, like goons.

Shame they managed to get us divided,

And it seems like it's no one's fault.

Poor Russia, my dear old homestead…

An unfailingly Eastern world.

In the letter to his friend S. Kusikov of 7 February 1923, Esenin wrote, *"I'm becoming despondent and struggling to make sense of this revolution I thought I belonged to. All I know is that it's no longer the 'February' or the 'October'. We need a 'November'."*[32]

Sadly, Esenin didn't live to see the new revolution he had been hoping for, as it never happened. Not the way he had hoped it would, anyway. Little did Esenin know, that the Germany he had referred to in that letter would launch a treacherous attack on his homeland in eighteen years' time.

But that is a sad and different story.

***

The last two years of Esenin's life were a constant (and

---

[32] Here Esenin was referring to the two Russian revolutions of 1917 – the February Bourgeois Democratic Revolution, and the subsequent Great October Revolution, both apparently failing to deliver on what had been promised. By 'November' Esenin must have meant a German nationalist uprising of 8-9 November, 1923, known as the Beer Hall Putsch; the failed attempt was directed against Germany's Weimar Republic's government.

exhausting) struggle against political harassment. Wherever he went, he would always end up involved in some sort of scandal or fight, usually (according to many eye-witnesses) started by someone else. A mere sneer from his companions or a derogatory remark from the crowd seemed enough to make the temperamental poet go up like a Roman candle. Routinely, each of these incidents would see Esenin escorted by the police to the nearest station - for a thorough interrogation by (this is important) the *Chekists*. Which begs the question: why were the secret police so concerned with what would normally have been deemed a public order offence and, as such, left to local civil enforcement officers to deal with? What was he really booked for time and time again? The answer is self-evident and it must be the poet himself.

On reflection, the seemingly unconnected events in Esenin's later years, as a whole, paint a curious, if not an ominous picture. *Maybe* the poisonous atmosphere of manhunt, desolation, and isolation (as in having no real confidants), was part of a furtive anti-Esenin campaign; *maybe, just maybe* – it was designed to eliminate the ideological foe; because how else does a hostile regime get rid of a poet who is so prominent and revered by the masses without directly or indirectly exposing itself? Whatever that anti-Esenin campaign was, it would have been enough to drive anyone to suicide, let alone the temperamental, sentimental, drinking type that Esenin was in later life. Anyone. But this is Esenin we're talking about.

So how did he really die? The following few pages may not be the most relaxing read for many of you, and I am not a particular fan of all things morbid myself. Yet some things must be told so that you the reader may draw your own conclusions.

***

Ironically, my very first acquaintance with Sergei Esenin and his poetry began with the story of his death; this was almost twenty years ago. It was another lesson on the poets of the Silver Age, with the featured poet being one Sergei Esenin.

My mother, a Russian Language and Literature

teacher, has always differed from her colleagues in her treatment of educational content. So instead of starting by giving us his lifespan and outline of major works, she intoned, "In the wee hours of the morning on the 28th December, 1925, a group of men filed out of the back entrance of the Hotel Angleterre, carrying something heavy wrapped in a rug. They dropped their burden on the sledge and started off along the still dark and empty St Petersburg streets. And as the sledge hit pothole after pothole on the road, so bounced on the sledge Esenin's once golden head…"

If my mother's vocation was not teaching, she would have probably made a great scriptwriter. For everyone in the class fell silent after that unexpected and somewhat macabre intro – even the usual class clowns.

And then my mother started reciting Esenin's poems - from memory. That's just how she rolls in class, well, she is an award-winning teacher of Russian Literature after all.

To this day, that lesson remains one of my most

memorable secondary school moments, and I am not saying this out of daughterly love. We all felt something during that lesson – a kind of connection to a real-life, a real human being, rather than a name in a textbook. To use a modern expression, us and Esenin just clicked.

The following week we were back in our Russian literature class with our homework. During my schooldays, homework checks in Russian schools were like this: the teacher would look at the grade book and call out a name, and that person would get up from their desk - and sometimes even come forward to where the teacher was sat - to present their homework in front of the rather relieved rest of us. The homework was usually the same for everyone, and the process was a bit like Russian roulette for those who hadn't bothered to study at home. That intense, thick silence as the teacher's pen moved slowly down the list of names in search of a 'victim' was an experience like no other!

That week's homework was one that nearly everyone, except myself (obviously), hated - poetry recital. Yet the number of volunteers was overwhelming, class clowns included. And so the whole time that we were supposed to be covering a new topic, we were just reciting Esenin's poems, one by one, and really rather enjoying ourselves.

This somewhat sentimental digression serves to illustrate the bond that we, who were then only teenagers, developed with the poet by simply listening to the story of his life. Even amongst the other, equally tragic fortunes of his fellow poets and contemporaries, Sergei Esenin's biography stood out and made the biggest impression on us – it was so real, almost tangible, and so sad, the Russian way.

MURDER OR SUICIDE?

In 2017, a major celebration of the centenary of the Great October Revolution was held in both Russia and the UK. Articles, TV documentaries, panel talks, and various other cultural activities on the subject abounded. Even *The Economist* ran a front cover featuring Vladimir Putin styled as an early twentieth-century Russian emperor.

While the general sentiment among British historians and Russophiles may be that the Revolution proved to be no bad thing for the country and the world after all, for Sergei Esenin it proved literally fatal.

Until very recently there has been practically no mention in English online sources of alternative versions of Esenin's death, besides the classic Soviet-era story (that he spiralled towards suicide due to his heavy drinking and debauching). Today, the largest and most popular general reference platform, Wikipedia, offers a large amount of information on a murder conspiracy, which, based on what I have read on the subject to date, I believe holds enough water to be dismissed out of hand.

For clarity, the version of Esenin's biography presented in this book is rather abbreviated and merely defines a frame of reference which might be used as a vantage point for understanding his poetry and behaviour; it is, therefore, by no means exhaustive or conclusive. I would urge any interested party to explore Sergei Esenin's life, work, and death in more detail online or in print.

***

I believe without question that there was more to Sergei Esenin's personal drama than just alcohol abuse and maladjustment to the realities of the changing world. Had he lived and worked a few decades later or earlier, he would most likely have ended up as someone else; he would have probably been less known now, less revered. It was the times he lived through that shaped him into the Esenin we can now Google freely.

Time is the greatest healer, but it is also a major killer. And what means of 'destruction' were at hand in the twentieth century? For Russia – two revolutions, two World Wars, and the Bolsheviks... all within the space of three decades. Merely three seconds on the timeline of the Universe.

In my mind, I combined the knowledge of Esenin's personal and lyrical legacy with what I had studied in literature lessons at school and what I have also read to date on Russian history. And this is where my train of thought has led me.

***

Sadly enough, Esenin's life-and-death story seems to be a pattern which has been applied to some outstanding artistic individuals in Russia for no one really knows how long. Igor Talkov, a prominent figure in the Soviet/Russian rock scene of the late '80s – early '90s (a chaotic time following the collapse of the Soviet Union), may well be the most recent and striking example of the covert oppression of charismatic poets on civic duty. Talkov's death is still considered purely accidental today, despite some rather fishy circumstances surrounding it. During a 1991 pop concert in St Petersburg (formerly Leningrad), he was shot and killed in a backstage row between his bodyguard and another singer's bodyguard – allegedly over which act was going to close the concert (apparently a big deal in the music world of that time). According to eye-witnesses, the row was instigated by Talkov's own impresario who, shortly after the incident, emigrated to the US, never to be contacted again by Talkov's circle. And Igor Talkov, like Esenin, had been really interested in Russian history and had written many essays and poems denouncing both the old (Soviet) and the new (post-Perestroika) regimes. Like Esenin's, Talkov's late verses were mostly patriotic and provocative.

***

Here is, in brief, my interpretation of what the times were like for Sergei Esenin's generation.

***

The overthrow of the Russian monarchy brought about a revolution in the Empire. Or rather it was the October Revolution of 1917 that caused the monarchy to topple. It would be fairer to say that, as always in history, these two events are inseparable and interconnected. It would take a hundred pages to speculate on the causes of either, and the speculation would be sure to stretch as far as World War I, or even further - into the succession of trials and tribulations that have always formed part of Russia's everyday life.

The Russians have never lived entirely happily. They have always been let down by the establishment – perhaps just like other parts of the world.

Indeed, we have only a few great politicians to boast about – the national heroes, the monumental figures shining through the dim and grim pages of the book that is the official history of Russia. Those were the early Princes of Kievan Rus who ruled at some point in the ninth to tenth centuries A.D., when what is known as Russia today was still a tiny patch on the map, torn by feudal rows and tribal wars.

Their names were Veshchij Oleg (veshchij - prophetic), who united Slavs and marched on the Byzantine Empire, and Yaroslav Mudriy (mudriy – wise), who completely devoted himself to educating the nation and encouraging general literacy through favouring books and arts, as well as Christian virtues.

Some might also name the eighteenth-century rulers Peter I and Catherine II - but to me they don't seem to embody all things Russian, in fact they do rather the opposite. Peter I (otherwise known as 'The Great') was obsessed with the European world and tried to model Russian life on it, and Catherine II (also nicknamed 'The Great') was a German princess who was baptised Ekaterina upon her arrival in Russia (as the future wife of Emperor Peter III). She still deserves a lot of credit for her genuine, unconditional devotion to the country that she would later call her only true home.

Having allowed myself this long and somewhat random flashback, I now only want to focus on the task at hand – that is to challenge the myth that is Sergei Esenin's suicide.

Being born into that époque (the early twentieth century) might be called a suicide in itself. Some people (Esenin among them) just knew it, sensed it, saw beyond it into a bigger picture; and it hurt to see and realise certain things, yet it couldn't be helped.

***

If I said that Esenin loved Russia, his Motherland, more than his own life, it would seem far too dramatic, to the point of becoming grotesque. But he did. He loved his ancient, Slavic, 'wooden' Russia; he loved his people, his language and folklore, and his culture. He loved every single thing about the place where he lived. Love is key, the key to understanding almost anything. Love is caring, sharing, participating. Putting that into the context of Esenin's life, Esenin cared for Russia and wanted to share the sufferings of his own people.

He longed for a change (even if it required a fundamental refurbishment of the whole system – as long as it made people happier, anything would do). He was an SR (member of the Social-Revolutionist party of the early 1900s). He fiercely supported the Revolution of 1905, which pursued the sole aim of limiting and weakening the Tsar's power by way of introducing constitutional freedoms. He was excited about the Great October Revolution as well – a different mood had been growing slowly for years, the frustration deepening in the masses, the working class and peasantry grieving about their harsh lives. Everyone wanted a change, but a change for the better, of course.

I mentioned before that Esenin documented his life in verse. So everything we need to know about Esenin's views and hopes is contained in his work. Maybe that is why he had been shut out for so long – in every way conceivable – from the minds of the Soviet people. His every verse was a prick of truth, and truth wasn't part of the vocabulary of that époque. His civil verses exposed, hurt, cut into the very nerves with an uncanny audacity – a sort of mad bravery spiked with deep melancholy and a sense of inevitable drama.

***

In the light of new evidence uncovered in recent years, it seems highly likely that Esenin may indeed have been assassinated, and his suicide staged. If that is true, it must have been a cruel, premeditated murder carried out to get rid of the unwanted poet - for numerous reasons. And he wasn't the only one to have been 'mistreated' by that day's establishment. Nikolai Gumilev, Maksim Gorky, Vladimir Mayakovsky, and Boris Pasternak may well have suffered directly or indirectly from the despotic, anti-Russian early-twentieth century Bolshevik regime that didn't tolerate dissent.

Boris Pasternak's own funeral, for one, nearly turned into a demonstration when the assembled Party officials managing the proceedings decided to end the ceremony abruptly after someone in the crowd had started reciting Pasternak's banned poem 'Hamlet'. And just before the ceremony, his wife Olga Ivinskaya talked to a family friend, writer Konstantin Paustovsky, who didn't seem to think much of poets' funerals, describing them as "so characteristic of the Russia which stoned its prophets and did its poets to death as a matter of longstanding tradition." (Quote source: Wikipedia).

***

Although Esenin had few illusions about tsarist rule, he didn't like the sight of a drunken crowd vandalising the former aristocrats' apartments in the centre of Imperial Saint Petersburg, either. When people started fighting with the tsarist époque relics, he knew that it would end in tears. Extremism of any sort repelled him. In his eyes, the crimes of the Tsarist regime didn't absolve the Bolsheviks' own government of plunging what used to be the Great Russian Empire into lawlessness. The grip on power of half-literate workmen, sailors, and former army recruits, united in an attempt to bring about a positive change by abolishing social classes, was resilient and reinforced by a group of quasi-socialist demagogues who may have been after quite a different thing altogether.

***

The aftermath of the Great October Revolution didn't reduce Esenin's civil workload. He was quick to see through Lenin's rhetoric (and those who came to power alongside him) that the people's expectations of a better and more equitable society would soon be crashing through the floor. For he had guessed at what the rhetoric actually masked – an unprecedented level of evil and brainwashing, Russophobia, oppression and even further enslavement. The regime imposed by the Bolsheviks was authoritarian and corrupt. The word 'criminal' may not be too far off, either. The Bolsheviks used the Russian people and their needs as a shield, a cover for all their lawless deeds and personal gain. In fact, they betrayed their people. It was all still there – famine, unemployment, crime, looting, prostitution, the general degradation of the masses (with a whole generation of aristocrats and intelligentsia exterminated, forced out of the country, or exiled in the course of the 'liberating' Revolution); and finally the Russian Civil War of 1917-1922.

The awakening from a 'sweet' socialist dream was a blow. And as Esenin wrote his major civil works (*'Land of Scoundrels'* and *'Pugachev'*), the government grew more and more concerned with him as a potential ideological threat. His message might have reached the unhappy, and yesterday's pro-Bolshevik crowds might become today's opponents. It was crucial that power should remain with the Party, and all potential threats were to be liquidated. As for the common people – they should be silenced, there and then. They should be shown the reigning regime's true colours, all of its might and wrath, so that the horror of what they saw should remove the slightest notion of resistance from their minds once and for all. And silence the people of Russia the Bolsheviks did. For the most in-demand Russian poet of that troubled period made a perfect 'burnt offering'.

**

… And so a popular folktale goes that early on the morning of December 28th, 1925, a group of police officers left the back entrance of the Hotel Angleterre in Isaakiy Square, St Petersburg, carrying Sergei Esenin's body which had been hastily rolled up in a piece of carpet from his room. In keeping with classical murder conspiracies, a great effort must have been made to prevent the body from being seen by both laymen and experts.

A series of books and articles by Eduard Klhystalov, a former KGB officer who conducted his own investigation after coming across Esenin's case in the state archives, offers a quite credible story of how the poet may have been assassinated. One of his book titles reads quite squarely: Как убили Сергея Есенина (How They Murdered Sergei Esenin).

Hit in the forehead with a blunt instrument... The characteristic strangulation marks on the neck betrayed the initial plan of his assassins to attack from behind and strangle him so that they could hang him from a heating pipe afterwards – a perfect suicide. Only he must have fought them off vigorously.

The ugly hole in the forehead – right between the eyebrows (which is clearly visible in the funeral photos) – would later be explained as a post-mortem trauma caused by Esenin's head hitting the hot pipe after his body had dropped and bounced in agonizing convulsions which are apparently typical of hanging.

This was how the body was found at the scene: a man hanging on a heating pipe in a somewhat awkward position, his right hand bent around the pipe, as if in an attempt to hold on to it, a worn-out leather belt sitting loosely on his neck.

Detailed descriptions of the place and the position of the body were made, photographs taken – but never revealed until around the last decade of the twentieth century, when the classified documents on Esenin's case, successfully stored away for over eighty years, were finally disclosed, and a bestselling book was written that inspired a TV-show *'Esenin'* featuring, among many leading Russian actors, Hollywood star Sean Young (as Isadora Duncan).

***

Soon after the police arrived, a black Voronok ('Little Raven' - the Bolsheviks' signature secret police vehicle) pulled up, and Cheka/OGPU officials took over the case - only to rule that the death was an apparent suicide, something that was pretty much expected of the riotous, miserable wreck that Esenin had so aggressively been labelled as for the last few years.

***

When my mother was a school girl, Esenin was still a

'taboo poet'; little was written about him in textbooks, and even less than half of that was probably true. When she grew up and became a Russian Literature teacher, she would tell her pupils about a different Esenin – a word guru, a rebel, a ladies' man, someone with a gift, a great poet and – most importantly – a patriot, in the most refined sense of the word. He could have chosen to glorify the new regime, he could have lived the life of the Party favourite – they needed his talent, the power of artistic persuasion weaved so elaborately into his verse. He could have made the perfect Herald of the Revolution.

Or, he could have lived comfortably with Isadora abroad, travelling around the world with her, enjoying a life of ease.

But there was Mother Russia, there were its people and they were as desperate as ever; they called for him, and he came back. He chose to share whatever gloomy fate delivered – together with his country and his fellow nationals. He returned to be the Herald of Truth, even knowing the price he was soon to pay for it, and dreading it secretly.

Esenin's circle would later reminisce about his fears and premonitions, and his general air of feeling hunted down. Some alleged confidants even stated that Esenin had known his assassins and that there had already been a few attempts on his life - but each time he would manage to escape, as there was always someone from his circle around...

And on that last evening of December 27th, 1925 – as the folktale goes - Esenin was entertaining some friends in his hotel suite. When the guests started to leave after dinner, he asked Wolf Erlich if he and his wife would care to stay the night. They refused – on the pretext of an important family business to tend to later that evening. Esenin made no further attempts to make them stay.

However Erlich returned, some twenty minutes later, to pick up a briefcase he had left – only to find Esenin sitting at his desk, his back to the door, quiet, writing. They said their goodbyes again and Erlich left. He later stressed in his memoirs that Esenin had looked suspiciously quiet and somewhat tired.

At the door, Erlich looked back at Esenin one last time – a silent, fur-coated (there had been some problems with central heating at the hotel) figure sitting at the desk. That was how Esenin must have spent his last hours, or minutes.

According to Khlystalov's story, Erlich was one of the Chekists (agents of the secret police); now it is up to the reader to choose whether to connect the dots.

***

There is one more thing to be said about Esenin's last night at the Hotel Angleterre; a detail which further cemented his lyrical image, adding a touch of legend to his life and death and placing him at the top of the twentieth-century Russian bohemian elite.

According to Wolf Erlich, the iconic poem *'Goodbye, my friend, it's time to leave'* [33] was Esenin's very last. He had complained to Erlich, the day before his death, that there was no ink in his room and that he had to write with his own blood. Was it a strange

---

[33] Also known in other translations as 'Goodbye, my friend, goodbye' and 'Farewell, my friend, farewell'

coincidence? Or a suicide attempt, perhaps? Would it make sense though, to cut your wrist open and then wait around almost twenty-four hours to eventually hang yourself – all the while writing a poem in between?

After all, if he did hang himself, why leave behind overturned, broken furniture, and the general appearance of a minor battlefield? Unless, of course, he intended to get into one final fight with his immediate surroundings before going. And according to the old photographs on hand, Esenin's hotel room was a real mess.

Those are the questions I will never be able to answer.

***

Erlich found a piece of paper with the poem in his coat pocket the following morning – but how and when Esenin had put it in there remains a mystery.

> *Goodbye, my friend, no hand, no sigh...*
> *Goodbye, my friend, and, please, don't grieve.*
> *In this life, it is not new to die.*
> *Much more is it common to live.**

It was written in blood.

When all is said and done, and the dice have been cast, that would seem to be a good way to go (by choice or not). One that will forever be a folktale, as Sergei Esenin truly was.

SELECTED POEMS
IN RUSSIAN AND ENGLISH

"Там, где капустные грядки...", 1910

Там, где капустные грядки
Красной водой поливает восход,
Кленёночек маленький матке
Зеленое вымя сосёт.

"Yonder, amid cabbage patches...", 1910

Yonder, amid cabbage patches,
Watered by light from the red rising dawn,
A small maple tree has found refuge
And feeds on the green teat of Earth.

"Вот уж вечер. Роса...", 1910

Вот уж вечер. Роса
Блестит на крапиве.
Я стою у дороги,
Прислонившись к иве.

От луны свет большой
Прямо на нашу крышу.
Где-то песнь соловья
Вдалеке я слышу.

Хорошо и тепло,
Как зимой у печки.
И берёзы стоят,
Как большие свечки.

И вдали за рекой,
Видно, за опушкой,
Сонный сторож стучит
Мёртвой колотушкой.

"Nightfall. Dew drops...", 1910

Nightfall. Dew drops
Make the nettle shimmer.
I am outside,
Back against a willow.

Moonlight floods rooftops;
Bright light, almost stinging.
In the distance beyond,
Nightingales are singing.

Feels so nice, feels so warm,
Much like in a cradle.
Birch trees lining the road,
Like some giant candles.

Down yonder, across
Streams and forest edges,
Sleepy woodman's awake
Singing forest praises.

"Выткался на озере алый свет зари...", 1910

Выткался на озере алый свет зари.
На бору со звонами плачут глухари.

Плачет где-то иволга, схоронясь в дупло.
Только мне не плачется — на душе светло.

Знаю, выйдешь к вечеру за кольцо дорог,
Сядем в копны свежие под соседний стог.

Зацелую допьяна, изомну, как цвет,
Хмельному от радости пересуду нет.

Ты сама под ласками сбросишь шелк фаты,
Унесу я пьяную до утра в кусты.

И пускай со звонами плачут глухари,
Есть тоска веселая в алостях зари.

"Dawn has spilt its crimson on the sleepy pond...",
1910

Dawn has spilt its crimson on the sleepy pond.
Grouses in the pinewood raise their sonant song.

From its nest, so dolefully, little red bird cries.
I don't feel like crying, for my heart is high.

For I know – at twilight you will come outside,
And we'll sit in soft mows of the fresh hay pile.

I will kiss you senseless, I will hug you wild.
Blame me not – I'm simply drunk on your sweet smile.

Yielding to my soft touch, you will whisper 'please...';
And the night will wrap us in its purple fleece.

Let the grouses warble their sonant song.
There's a joyful sadness in the hugs of dawn.

"Звезды", 1911

Звёздочки ясные, звёзды высокие!
Что вы храните в себе, что скрываете?
Звёзды, таящие мысли глубокие,
Силой какою вы душу пленяете?

Частые звёздочки, звёздочки тесные!
Что в вас прекрасного, что в вас могучего?
Чем увлекаете, звёзды небесные,
Силу великую знания жгучего?

И почему так, когда вы сияете,
Маните в небо, в объятья широкие?
Смотрите нежно так, сердце ласкаете,
Звёзды небесные, звёзды далекие!

"Stars", 1911

Stars, little stars, you're so high and so bright!
What is that secret that you have been keeping?
Stars, full of thoughts so deep and profound,
    Why is your power just so captivating?

Stars, little stars, so frequent and close!
What is your beauty, and what is your might?
What's that about you that simply enthrals,
    Offering wisdom and knowledge of life?

Why is your beaming so tempting and welcoming,
Beaconing gently, embracing and cherishing?
When you look down, our hearts are awakening,
    You are so far away, yet so congenial!

"Весенний вечер", 1911-12

Тихо струится река серебристая
В царстве вечернем зелёной весны.
Солнце садится за горы лесистые.
Рог золотой выплывает луны.

Запад подернулся лентою розовой,
Пахарь вернулся в избушку с полей,
И за дорогою, в чаще берёзовой,
Песню любви затянул соловей.

Слушает ласково песни глубокие
С запада розовой лентой заря.
С нежностью смотрит на звёзды далекие
И улыбается небу земля.

"An Evening in Spring", 1911-12

Quietly ripples the river of silver
In the night kingdom of luscious, green spring.
Sun lowers over the hills, dark and sylvan.
Golden-horned moon sails out of the mist.

Pink light has flooded the westerly skyline,
Ploughman returned to his hut from the fields.
Over the country lane, deep in the birch wilds,
Amorous nightingales started to sing.

Westerly pink hovers over the landscape,
Listening softly to those deep-fetched tunes.
Earth gazes longingly into the starry space,
Smiling at those distant planets and moons.

"Береза", 1913

Белая берёза
Под моим окном
Принакрылась снегом,
Точно серебром.

На пушистых ветках
Снежною каймой
Распустились кисти
Белой бахромой.

И стоит берёза
В сонной тишине,
И горят снежинки
В золотом огне.

А заря, лениво
Обходя кругом,
Обсыпает ветки
Новым серебром.

"The Birch Tree", 1913

There is a birch tree
Right under my window,
All covered in snow,
As if in real silver.

And the fluffy branches,
Set with snowy fringe,
Blossom in white bunches,
Full to the brim.

And the birch tree stands
In the sleepy silence,
And the snowflakes burn
In the golden fire.

And the lazy dawn,
Walking round the tree,
Sprinkles the branches
With more silver beads.

"Песнь о собаке", 1915

Утром в ржаном закуте,
Где златятся рогожи в ряд,
Семерых ощенила сука,
Рыжих семерых щенят.
До вечера она их ласкала,
Причёсывая языком,
И струился снежок подталый
Под тёплым ее животом.

А вечером, когда куры
Обсиживают шесток,
Вышел хозяин хмурый,
Семерых всех поклал в мешок.
По сугробам она бежала,
Поспевая за ним бежать…
И так долго, долго дрожала
Воды незамерзшей гладь.

А когда чуть плелась обратно,
Слизывая пот с боков,
Показался ей месяц над хатой
Одним из её щенков.

В синюю высь звонко
Глядела она, скуля,
А месяц скользил тонкий
И скрылся за холм в полях.

И глухо, как от подачки,
Когда бросят ей камень в смех,
Покатились глаза собачьи
Золотыми звёздами в снег.

"Ode to the Dog", 1915

In the morning, inside a rye barn,
Stacked full of golden burlaps,
A she-dog gave birth to a litter
Of seven little red pups.
Till dusk she was nuzzling her babies,
Combing their coats with her tongue.
And the snow under her warm belly
Was melting into the ground.

And at night, when the tired chickens
Doze off on the hencoop rack,
Out came the gloomy dog's owner
And put all the pups in a sack.
Over snowdrifts she chased her owner,
Struggling to keep pace…
And for long afterwards couldn't settle
The lake's broken icy expanse.

And when doddering back to her kennel,
Licking sweat off her aching legs,
In the new moon above the house,
She saw one of her little whelps.

Long and hard did she stare and howl
At the moon in the deep blue sky…
But the moon lowered over a hillside
And sailed out of sight.

With a thud of a heavy stone,
Hurled at her many times in the past,
The poor old dog's tears
Came down, like shooting stars.

"Вечер, как сажа, льется в окно...", 1914-16

Вечер, как сажа,
Льётся в окно.
Белая пряжа
Ткёт полотно.

Пляшет гасница,
Прыгает тень.
В окна стучится
Старый плетень.

Липнет к окошку
Чёрная гать.
Девочку-крошку
Байкает мать.

Взрыкает зыбка
Сонный тропарь:
"Спи, моя рыбка,
Спи, не гутарь".

"Night-time creeps in, pitch black, like grime...", *1914-16*

Night-time creeps in -
Pitch black, like grime.
In through the window -
White canvas of yarn.

Candlestick dancing,
Shadows awake.
Wicker fence tapping
On window frames.

Darkness around, like mud -
Black and deep.
Mother is lulling
Her baby to sleep.

Drowsy movements,
Bleary eyes:
'Hush, little baby,
Hush, don't you cry.'

"Корова", 1915

Дряхлая, выпали зубы,
Свиток годов на рогах.
Бил её выгонщик грубый
На перегонных полях.

Сердце неласково к шуму,
Мыши скребут в уголке.
Думает грустную думу
О белоногом телке.

Не дали матери сына,
Первая радость не впрок.
И на колу под осиной
Шкуру трепал ветерок.

Скоро на гречневом свее,
С той же сыновней судьбой,
Свяжут ей петлю на шее
И поведут на убой.

Жалобно, грустно и тоще
В землю вопьются рога…
Снится ей белая роща
И травяные луга.

"The Cow", 1915

Wintery, now almost toothless,
Horns streaked with years of hard graft.
From people she's seen only rudeness,
Migrating from grass to grass.

Heart swarmed with pain and uneasy,
Mice scrabbling in the dark.
With one thing her mind is busy –
Her little white-legged calf.

Her first motherhood was flashy,
The calf got taken away.
Under the windy aspens,
His skin flapped, attached to a stake.

Soon she'll be joined by her littlun,
When from the buckwheat grounds
She will be noosed by the herdsman
Straight to the slaughterhouse.

So dolefully, into the ground,
Will sink her fragile horns…
She's dreaming about lush greenland,
And picturesque white groves.

"Лисица",
А.М. Ремизову, 1915

На раздробленной ноге приковыляла,
У норы свернулася в кольцо.
Тонкой прошвой кровь отмежевала
На снегу дремучее лицо.

Ей все бластился в колючем дыме выстрел,
Колыхалася в глазах лесная топь.
Из кустов косматый ветер взбыстрил
И рассыпал звонистую дробь.

Как желна, над нею мгла металась.
Мокрый вечер липок был и ал.
Голова тревожно подымалась,
И язык на ране застывал.

Жёлтый хвост упал в метель пожаром.
На губах — как прелая морковь…
Пахло инеем и глиняным угаром,
А в ощур сочилась тихо кровь.

"The Vixen"
To A.M. Remizov, 1915

On her broken leg the vixen scrambled,
By the burrow, rolled into a ball.
With saccadic lines her blood had painted
Weird shapes on freshly-fallen snow.

She kept hearing the shot and smelling gun smoke,
Forest bog still waffed before her eyes.
Villous wind flew out of the coppice,
Carrying with it the hollow sounds.

Darkness tossed about, like a raven,
Soggy night was clammy and maroon.
She kept looking up, suddenly scared,
And her tongue would stop licking the wound.

Orange tail set the snow on fire,
Reddish tint on lips - sticky and dark.
She lay there, breathing frost and mire,
While her body slowly drained of blood.

Мальвине Мироновне, 1916

В глазах пески зелёные
И облака.
По кружеву крапленому
Скользит рука.

То близкая, то дальняя,
И так всегда.
Судьба её печальная —
Моя беда.

To Malvina Mironovna, 1916

Her eyes are sands of green,
The cloudbank.
The silky filigree
Nurses my hand.

Now close to me, now far -
Always the way.
Her gloomy fate, her plight -
My pain.

"В зеленой церкви за горой…", 1916,
Константиново

В зелёной церкви за горой,
Где вербы четки уронили,
Я поминаю просфорой
Младой весны младые были.

А ты, склонившаяся ниц,
Передо мной стоишь незримо,
Шелка опущенных ресниц
Колышут крылья херувима.

Не омрачён твой белый рок
Твоей застывшею порою,
Всё тот же розовый платок
Затянут смуглою рукою.

Всё тот же вздох упруго жмёт
Твои надломленные плечи
О том, кто за морем живет
И кто от родины далече.

И всё тягуче память дня
Перед пристойным ликом жизни.
О, помолись и за меня,
За бесприютного в отчизне.

"A small green church over the hills...", 1916, Konstantinovo village

A small green church, over the hills,
Where willows bow, as if in prayer;
The place I go to mourn my dreams,
My youthful past, my joyful manner.

And in my mind, I see you there,
The humble form I deem so precious.
Winged cherubs must have weaved from air
The luscious silk of your eyelashes.

Your hallowed life is safe from grief,
And as you kneel down in devotion,
I contemplate your pink kerchief,
Your swarthy hand, your gentle motions.

You'll heave a mournful, lasting sigh,
And drop your grieving, sunken shoulders.
For all those gone into the night
You'll pray till day fades into smoulders.

The memories of the day gone by
Stand there, like a mental burden.
Oh, do be kind and pray for me,
A stranger in my own homeland.

"День ушел, убавилась черта…", 1916

День ушёл, убавилась черта,
Я опять подвинулся к уходу.
Легким взмахом белого перста
Тайны лет я разрезаю воду.

В голубой струе моей судьбы
Накипи холодной бьётся пена
И кладёт печать немого плена
Складку новую у сморщенной губы.

С каждым днём я становлюсь чужим
И себе, и жизнь кому велела.
Где-то в поле чистом, у межи,
Оторвал я тень свою от тела.

Неодетая она ушла,
Взяв мои изогнутые плечи.
Где-нибудь она теперь далече
И другого нежно обняла.

Может быть, склоняяся к нему,
Про меня она совсем забыла
И, вперившись в призрачную тьму,
Складки губ и рта переменила.

Но живёт по звуку прежних лет,
Что, как эхо, бродит за горами.
Я целую синими губами
Чёрной тенью тиснутый портрет.

"Night again, another day is off...", 1916

Night again, another day is off,
I am one step closer to departure.
Cautiously, my pointer finger waffs,
Piercing the unknown, like an archer.

In the light-blue stream that is my life,
Frosty scum is spuming in defiance,
Casting its oppressive spell of silence
On my wrinkled and distorted mouth.

Day by day, I slowly move away
From myself and everyone who knows me.
In the plough fields, by a forest glade,
I detached my shadow from my body.

And my naked shadow then made off,
Carrying with it my sunken shoulders.
It must now be far away and older,
And has someone else to gently fold.

Maybe I'm no longer on its mind,
Every time it leans towards its keeper.
Staring into the ghostly night,
Maybe it has flattened their wrinkles.

But I know it might one day turn back,
Like a rambling echo in the hills.
I am kissing with my bluish lips
The beloved portrait edged in black.

"Вот такой, какой есть...", 1919

Вот такой, какой есть,
Никому ни в чём не уважу,
Золотою плету я песнь,
А лицо иногда в сажу.

Говорят, что я большевик.
Да, я рад зауздать землю.
О, какой богомаз мои лик
Начертил, грозовице внемля?

Пусть Америка, Лондон пусть...
Разве воды текут обратно?
Это пляшет российская грусть,
На солнце смывая пятна.

"I am just what I am...", 1919

I am just what I am;
Not doing anyone favours,
I am known to talk a good game,
But sometimes I can also be shameless.

They say I am Bolshevik.
Yes, I'd like to see land bridled.
Oh, whoever created me
Was sick, or otherwise kidding.

London, New York – same to me...
Can rivers ever flow backwards?
Watch a boisterous Russian grief
Shooting up for the sun, like crackers.

"Исповедь хулигана", 1920

Не каждый умеет петь,
Не каждому дано яблоком
Падать к чужим ногам.

Сие есть самая великая исповедь,
Которой исповедуется хулиган.

Я нарочно иду нечёсаным,
С головой, как керосиновая лампа, на плечах.
Ваших душ безлиственную осень
Мне нравится в потемках освещать.
Мне нравится, когда каменья брани
Летят в меня, как град рыгающей грозы,
Я только крепче жму тогда руками
Моих волос качнувшийся пузырь.

Так хорошо тогда мне вспоминать
Заросший пруд и хриплый звон ольхи,
Что где-то у меня живут отец и мать,
Которым наплевать на все мои стихи,
Которым дорог я, как поле и как плоть,
Как дождик, что весной взрыхляет зеленя.
Они бы вилами пришли вас заколоть
За каждый крик ваш, брошенный в меня.
Бедные, бедные крестьяне!
Вы, наверно, стали некрасивыми,
Так же боитесь бога и болотных недр.
О, если б вы понимали,
Что сын ваш в России
Самый лучший поэт!
Вы ль за жизнь его сердцем не индевели,
Когда босые ноги он в лужах осенних макал?

"Confession of a Hooligan", 1920

Not everyone knows how to sing,
Not everyone was born to fall,
Like an apple, at someone's feet.

This is the most sincere confession
Ever made by a deadbeat.

I look ill and scruffy on purpose,
My blonde head like a lamp on my shoulders.
In the darkness of bare autumn,
I shed light on your trivial souls.
I like it when abuse, like stones,
Comes down on me, spewed by a raging storm;
It only seems to make me stronger
So I can still be in top form.

I often reminisce at times like that
About the unkept pond, the ancient alder-tree.
It gives me peace to know my mum and dad
Are always there, loving me for me.
They couldn't care less what poetry I write,
They treasure me the same as their plough field,
They'd pitchfork anyone, without a doubt,
For every insult ever hurled at me.
Oh, poor, poor villagers!
You must have turned so ugly;
Still fearing your God, and marshland depths.
Oh, I so wish you knew, my dear ones,
That your fellow peasant
Is one of Russia's hot new poets!
Didn't it give you a fright, when he was growing up,
To see him tread on autumn puddles barefoot?

А теперь он ходит в цилиндре
И лакированных башмаках.

Но живёт в нем задор прежней вправки
Деревенского озорника.
Каждой корове с вывески мясной лавки
Он кланяется издалека.
И, встречаясь с извозчиками на площади,
Вспоминая запах навоза с родных полей,
Он готов нести хвост каждой лошади,
Как венчального платья шлейф.

Я люблю родину.
Я очень люблю родину!
Хоть есть в ней грусти ивовая ржавь.
Приятны мне свиней испачканные морды
И в тишине ночной звенящий голос жаб.
Я нежно болен вспоминаньем детства,
Апрельских вечеров мне снится хмарь и сырь.
Как будто бы на корточки погреться
Присел наш клён перед костром зари.
О, сколько я на нём яиц из гнёзд вороньих,
Карабкаясь по сучьям, воровал!
Всё тот же ль он теперь, с верхушкою зеленой?
По-прежнему ль крепка его кора?

А ты, любимый,
Верный пегий пес?!
От старости ты стал визглив и слеп
И бродишь по двору, влача обвисший хвост,
Забыв чутьём, где двери и где хлев.
О, как мне дороги все те проказы,
Когда, у матери стянув краюху хлеба,
Кусали мы с тобой её по разу,

Now he walks around in a top hat,
And patent boots.

But he still has inside him the ardour
Of a village wild child.
Every cow from a butcher's signboard
He bows to from afar.
And when seeing cabbies at the square,
Remembering the dung smell of native plough land,
He wants to carry every horse's tail,
Like they carry a wedding dress train.

I love my motherland.
I dote on my motherland!
Although it's full of rusty, mellow grief.
It pleases me to see pigs' mucky snouts
And hear froglets' quacking night motif.
I suffer from a delicate nostalgia,
Dreaming about cold, wet nights in spring.
As if to have a warm by daybreak fire,
Had squatted our good old maple tree.
How many times I'd climb its mighty boughs
To steal some eggs from poor crows' nests!
I wonder if it's shed its thick green crown,
And if its bark is still robust.

And you, my lovely,
Loyal, skewbald dog?!
Turned blind with age, your bark now just a whine.
You ramble round the yard, your tail down,
Forgetting where's home and where's barn.
Those dear little monkey tricks of mine,
When having stolen treats from mother's larder,
We'd share a good bite of tasty buns,

Ни капельки друг другом не погребав.

Я всё такой же.
Сердцем я всё такой же.
Как васильки во ржи, цветут в лице глаза.
Стеля стихов злачёные рогожи,
Мне хочется вам нежное сказать.

Спокойной ночи!
Всем вам спокойной ночи!
Отзвенела по траве сумерек зари коса...
Мне сегодня хочется очень
Из окошка луну ....*

Синий свет, свет такой синий!
В эту синь даже умереть не жаль.
Ну так что ж, что кажусь я циником,
Прицепившим к заднице фонарь!
Старый, добрый, заезженный Пегас,
Мне ль нужна твоя мягкая рысь?
Я пришёл, как суровый мастер,
Воспеть и прославить крыс.
Башка моя, словно август,
Льётся бурливых волос вином.

Я хочу быть жёлтым парусом
В ту страну, куда мы плывём.

Not being squeamish once about each other.

I'm still the same.
At heart, I'm still the same.
My eyes like bluets in a field of rye.
Stacking my verses, like they stack gilt hay,
I long to tell you something nice.

Sweet dreams!
Sweet dreams to everyone!
The scythe of dusk quit mowing for the night…
And tonight, of all nights, I feel like
Baying* at the moon in the sky.

Blue moonlight, such rich, blue moonlight!
Don't mind dying on a night like this!
So what if I act like a cynic,
Who stuck a lamp to his ass!
Good old worn-out Pegasus,
Think I need your unhurried pace?
I came, like a rugged master,
To praise and glorify rats.
My cabbage-head the colour of ale
Tumbles down like a castle of sand.

I want to be a yellow sail
On that ship to the 'Promised Land'.**

---

* Esenin deliberately omitted this verb, which was apparently a swear word -
on the fair assumption that native Russian speakers would guess at it based
on the alternate rhyme. I chose a different verb to complete the picture
without affecting the overall mood of the fragment. **The word-for-word
translation of this line would be: "[On that ship] to the country of our final
destination", meaning the country/land of socialism/communism.

"Мир таинственный, мир мой древний…", 1921

Мир таинственный, мир мой древний,
Ты, как ветер, затих и присел.
Вот сдавили за шею деревню
Каменные руки шоссе.

Так испуганно в снежную выбель
Заметалась звенящая жуть.
Здравствуй ты, моя чёрная гибель,
Я навстречу к тебе выхожу!

Город, город, ты в схватке жестокой
Окрестил нас как падаль и мразь.
Стынет поле в тоске волоокой,
Телеграфными столбами давясь.

Жилист мускул у дьявольской выи,
И легка ей чугунная гать.
Ну, да что же? Ведь нам не впервые
И расшатываться и пропадать.

Пусть для сердца тягуче колко,
Это песня звериных прав!..
… Так охотники травят волка,
Зажимая в тиски облав.

Зверь припал… и из пасмурных недр
Кто-то спустит сейчас курки…
Вдруг прыжок… и двуногого недруга
Раздирают на части клыки.

"Ancient world, my mysterious world...", 1921

Ancient world, my mysterious world,
Like the wind, you're so quiet and sad.
Look – the countryside's neck is squashed
By motorways' stone hands.

Like a killer snowstorm on a mission,
Rushed about the jingling dread...
Hi, you're there, my fatal destruction,
I've come out to meet you myself!

Oh, Big City, you're fighting against us,
And to you, we're but offal and scum.
Fields are drowning in cow-eyed sadness,
Choking on telegraph stumps.

Look how strong is this devilish bastard,
Paving fields with cast-iron log-roads.
Well, so what? It is not for the first time
That we've had to be ruined or lost.

I don't know if my meek heart can stand this,
Being chased by your pleading sobs.
...We're like wolves that are baited by hunters
And viciously viced by dogs.

See that wolf? He's so tense and so quiet,
As if waiting for guns to go off...
Then – a jump... and his teeth, quick as lightning,
Tear up the two-legged foe.

О, привет тебе, зверь мой любимый!
Ты не даром даешься ножу!
Как и ты — я отвсюду гонимый,
Средь железных врагов прохожу.

Как и ты — я всегда наготове,
И хоть слышу победный рожок,
Но отпробует вражеской крови
Мой последний, смертельный прыжок.

И пускай я на рыхлую выбель
Упаду и зароюсь в снегу…
Все же песню отмщенья за гибель
Пропоют мне на том берегу.

Oh, hello, wild beast, my beloved!
There's a reason you act like this then!
Just like you, I am always chased out,
And besieged by my iron foemen.

Just like you, I am always ready,
And despite the triumphant toot,
I will not stop attacking the enemy,
Even if it's the last thing I do.

Even if I come down, stunned and frightened,
To be buried in crumby snow...
You will hear a song of requital
Sung for me at the other shore.

"Песнь о хлебе", 1921

Вот она, суровая жестокость,
Где весь смысл — страдания людей!
Режет серп тяжелые колосья,
Как под горло режут лебедей.

Наше поле издавна знакомо
С августовской дрожью поутру.
Перевязана в снопы солома,
Каждый сноп лежит, как жёлтый труп.

На телегах, как на катафалках,
Их везут в могильный склеп — овин.
Словно дьякон, на кобылу гаркнув,
Чтит возница погребальный чин.

А потом их бережно, без злости,
Головами стелют по земле
И цепами маленькие кости
Выбивают из худых телес.

Никому и в голову не встанет,
Что солома — это тоже плоть!..
Людоедке-мельнице — зубами
В рот суют те кости обмолоть.

И, из мелева заквашивая тесто,
Выпекают груды вкусных яств…
Вот тогда-то входит яд белесый
В жбан желудка яйца злобы класть.

"Song of the Bread", 1921

There it is, the iron-handed grimness,
Symbolising torments of the world:
Sickle cutting off the golden wheat heads,
Like they cut the necks of lovely swans.

Every August gives us all a quiver,
What a mournful sight we must behold!
Plough fields are all strewn with golden wheat sheaves,
Every sheaf is like a yellow corpse.

Loaded onto horse-drawn waggon-hearses,
Sheaves are brought to their crypt – the barn.
Like a deacon, the obscure coachman
Spurs the horse with his lamenting chants.

At the barn, the sheaves' little, lean bodies
Are then stacked with care on the ground.
And the poor, tiny golden grain-bones
Get into the chains' hands - to be trounced.

It occurs to no one, for some reason,
That to wheat – its straw is same as flesh!...
That the ogre-mill will then be given
The ill-fated bones of wheat - to thresh.

Once the poor dough has been fermented,
They will bake a lot of tasty treats…
This is when the whitish poison enters
Our guts - to lay its eggs of spleen.

Все побои ржи в припёк окрасив,
Грубость жнущих сжав в духмяный сок,
Он вкушающим соломенное мясо
Отравляет жернова кишок.

И свистят по всей стране, как осень,
Шарлатан, убийца и злодей…
Оттого, что режет серп колосья,
Как под горло режут лебедей.

Passing off all beatings, pain and torment
For the bread's delicious golden crust,
This white killer acts the same as dead meat,
Poisoning and spoiling people's guts.

My beloved land is sieged by raw dregs:
Pettifoggers, villains and cutthroats...
All because the sickle cuts the wheat heads,
Like they cut the necks of lovely swans.

"Не жалею, не зову, не плачу…", 1921

Не жалею, не зову, не плачу,
Всё пройдёт, как с белых яблонь дым.
Увяданья золотом охваченный,
Я не буду больше молодым.

Ты теперь не так уж будешь биться,
Сердце, тронутое холодком,
И страна берёзового ситца
Не заманит шляться босиком.

Дух бродяжий, ты всё реже, реже
Расшевеливаешь пламень уст.
О, моя утраченная свежесть,
Буйство глаз и половодье чувств.

Я теперь скупее стал в желаньях,
Жизнь моя, иль ты приснилась мне?
Словно я весенней гулкой ранью
Проскакал на розовом коне.

Все мы, все мы в этом мире тленны,
Тихо льётся с клёнов листьев медь…
Будь же ты вовек благословенно,
Что пришло процвесть и умереть.

"No regrets, no entreating, no crying...", 1921

No regrets, no entreating, no crying.
All will pass, like bloom off apple trees.
Trapped in that autumnal swirl of dying,
I'll be young again no more, you see.

You'll be beating now, I guess, much slower,
Heart of mine, convulsed with evening cool.
Sorry, dear land of birch-tree cotton,
No more aimless roaming barefoot.

My once-weariless, roving spirit,
You're no longer making my heart move.
I am almost done trying to feel it,
Oh, my long-lost sap, my dew of youth.

There is nothing left for me to pine for,
Did I live at all or did I dream?
As if I had jovially galloped
Through the morning, pink-glazed furrowed field.

Everything and everyone will perish,
Maple trees have shed their copper glow...
May you then be praised and blessed forever
What was born to blossom and die off.

Всё живое особой метой
Отмечается с ранних пор.
Если не был бы я поэтом,
То, наверно, был мошенник и вор.

Худощавый и низкорослый,
Средь мальчишек всегда герой,
Часто, часто с разбитым носом
Приходил я к себе домой.

И навстречу испуганной маме
Я цедил сквозь кровавый рот:
«Ничего! Я споткнулся о камень,
Это к завтраму всё заживет».

И теперь вот, когда простыла
Этих дней кипятковая вязь,
Беспокойная, дерзкая сила
На поэмы мои пролилась.

Золотая, словесная груда,
И над каждой строкой без конца
Отражается прежняя удаль
Забияки и сорванца.
Как тогда, я отважный и гордый,
Только новью мой брызжет шаг...
Если раньше мне били в морду,
То теперь вся в крови душа.
И уже говорю я не маме,
А в чужой и хохочущий сброд:
«Ничего! Я споткнулся о камень,
Это к завтраму всё заживет!»

"All things living subconsciously know it...", 1922

All things living subconsciously know it:
There's a special mark on their souls.
If I hadn't become a poet,
I would now be a thief or a fraud.

Spare-built, somewhat vertically challenged,
The first teaser among the boys,
Many times I'd end up – to my pleasure -
Coming home with a bleeding nose.

In reply to my mum's troubled groan,
I would speak through the bleeding mouth:
"Never mind! I tripped over a stone,
By tomorrow it all will be fine."

And today, when I'm no longer driven
By the heat of my wild past,
An insolent, restless vigour
Splashed so suddenly onto my rhymes.

Golden words stacked in huge piles.
And invariably, in each word,
I can see the foregone prowess
Of the teaser I once was.
I am still as courageous and prideful,
Only swagger has changed somewhat...
If before I'd be punched in the muzzle,
Now they're thrashing my very soul.
Not at mummy my brag is now thrown,
But at all those guffawing lowlifes:
"Never mind! I tripped over a stone,
By tomorrow it all will be fine. "

"Не ругайтесь. Такое дело!", 1922

Не ругайтесь. Такое дело!
Не торговец я на слова.
Запрокинулась и отяжелела
Золотая моя голова.

Нет любви ни к деревне, ни к городу,
Как же смог я её донести?
Брошу всё. Отпущу себе бороду
И бродягой пойду по Руси.

Позабуду поэмы и книги,
Перекину за плечи суму,
Оттого что в полях забулдыге
Ветер больше поёт, чем кому.

Провоняю я редькой и луком
И, тревожа вечернюю гладь,
Буду громко сморкаться в руку
И во всём дурака валять.

И не нужно мне лучшей удачи,
Лишь забыться и слушать пургу,
Оттого что без этих чудачеств
Я прожить на земле не могу.

"Don't be down on me! You know nothing!", 1922

Don't be down on me! You know nothing!
Unlike you, I am cautious with words.
My once golden head has much suffered,
And turned heavy and numb, like frost.

No love left for the village and city,
How on earth could it be preserved?
And to hell with it. I'll grow a beard
And go roam, like a vagabond.

I'll forget about books, and my poems,
I'll set off with not more than a tote,
For I know - out there, in the forest,
Drunks like me find their perfect abode.

I'll be stinking of onions and turnips,
And upsetting the evening peace,
Will be honking right into my shirt sleeves,
And making a fool of myself.

And I don't need a better fortune
Than a nap to the sounds of snowfall,
For without these bees in my bonnet,
I don't know how to live in this world.

Вечер чёрные брови насопил,
Чьи-то кони стоят у двора.
Не вчера ли я молодость пропил?
Разлюбил ли тебя не вчера?

Не храпи, запоздалая тройка!
Наша жизнь пронеслась без следа.
Может, завтра больничная койка
Упокоит меня навсегда.

Может, завтра совсем по-другому
Я уйду, исцелённый навек,
Слушать песни дождей и черемух,
Чем здоровый живет человек.

Позабуду я мрачные силы,
Что терзали меня, губя.
Облик ласковый! Облик милый!
Лишь одну не забуду тебя.

Пусть я буду любить другую,
Но и с нею, с любимой, с другой,
Расскажу про тебя, дорогую,
Что когда-то я звал дорогой.

Расскажу, как текла былая
Наша жизнь, что былой не была...
Голова ль ты моя удалая,
До чего ж ты меня довела?

"Evening knitted its bushy black eyebrows…", 1923

Evening knitted its bushy black eyebrows.
Someone's horses are parked in the yard.
Did I drink up my youth in the days passed?
Did I stop loving you just last night?

Roar not, my poor old horses!
Our lives have gone by —not a trace.
And tomorrow I may find some solace
In one of those hospital beds.

And who knows - at the start of tomorrow,
Healed for good, I may pack up and leave
For the music of rain and bird-cherry
That helps people to breathe and to live.

I'll get over the sinister forces
That had tortured me year after year.
But the sweet face, your dearest sweet face
Will I keep in my memory always.

I may love someone else in the future,
But I'll tell that new girlfriend of mine
All about you, my lovely sweet cookie,
That I once called my darling, my one.

I will tell her of all that we'd shared
In the past – which has not even been…
Shame on me! Poor me… Damn it!
What has happened to poor old me?

Заметался пожар голубой,
Позабылись родимые дали.
В первый раз я запел про любовь,
В первый раз отрекаюсь скандалить.

Был я весь — как запущенный сад,
Был на женщин и зелие падкий.
Разонравилось пить и плясать
И терять свою жизнь без оглядки.

Мне бы только смотреть на тебя,
Видеть глаз злато-карий омут,
И чтоб, прошлое не любя,
Ты уйти не смогла к другому.

Поступь нежная, легкий стан,
Если б знала ты сердцем упорным,
Как умеет любить хулиган,
Как умеет он быть покорным.

Я б навеки забыл кабаки
И стихи бы писать забросил,
Только б тонко касаться руки
И волос твоих цветом в осень.

Я б навеки пошел за тобой
Хоть в свои, хоть в чужие дали…
В первый раз я запел про любовь,
В первый раз отрекаюсь скандалить.

"Feelings rage like a burning stove…", 1923

Feelings rage, like a burning stove,
My sweet home can no longer give solace.
It's my first ever song about love,
No more drinking and brawling, I promise.

I was then pretty ragged and lost,
Prone to playing around and drinking.
All that's gone, and the thing I'd hate most
Would be wasting my life without thinking.

I just want to behold your sweet eyes,
Getting lost in their hazel vortex,
So that you wouldn't leave me behind,
For a new love of yours – as a protest.

Lightweight footstep and slender frame,
Oh, I so wish you would know deep down
How a hooligan can be tame,
When he loves – love can make him humble.

Drunken riots would come to an end,
I would even give up writing poems
So that I could just touch your hand
And caress your soft locks painted autumn.

And I know I'd forever be yours,
Where you went I'd always shadow…
It's my first ever song about love,
No more drinking and brawling, I swear.

"Грубым дается радость", 1923

Грубым даётся радость,
Нежным даётся печаль.
Мне ничего не надо,
Мне никого не жаль.
Жаль мне себя немного,
Жалко бездомных собак.
Эта прямая дорога
Меня привела в кабак.

Что ж вы ругаетесь, дьяволы?
Иль я не сын страны?
Каждый из нас закладывал
За рюмку свои штаны.

Мутно гляжу на окна,
В сердце тоска и зной.
Катится, в солнце измокнув,
Улица передо мной.

А на улице мальчик сопливый.
Воздух поджарен и сух.
Мальчик такой счастливый
И ковыряет в носу.

Ковыряй, ковыряй, мой милый,
Суй туда палец весь,
Только вот с эфтой силой
В душу свою не лезь.
Я уж готов... Я робкий...
Глянь на бутылок рать!
Я собираю пробки —
Душу мою затыкать.

"Toughies are always mirthful…", 1923

Toughies are always mirthful,
Softies are always down.
I am in need of nothing
And feeling for no one.
Myself I do pity a little,
The same as I do stray dogs.
This is exactly the reason
Why I have turned a sot.

Why are you cursing, devils?
Ain't I the son of my land?
Everyone once was prepared
To pawn - for a shot - their slacks.

Looking at windows dimly,
Heart full of thirst and heat.
Scorched in the sunny pinwheel,
The street rolls in front of me.

In the street, there's a snotty munchkin.
The air is dry and frail.
The munchkin just looks so happy,
Picking his nose away.

Carry on, pick it hard, my dear,
Shove your finger in all the way.
Only don't use the same vigour
Reaching into your inner self.
There I am… quite tipsy and milktoast…
Look at this bottle crowd!
I am collecting wine corks –
To bottle up my heart.

Дорогая, сядем рядом…", 1923

Дорогая, сядем рядом,
Поглядим в глаза друг другу.
Я хочу под кротким взглядом
Слушать чувственную вьюгу.

Это золото осенье,
Эта прядь волос белесых —
Всё явилось, как спасенье
Беспокойного повесы.

Я давно мой край оставил,
Где цветут луга и чащи.
В городской и горькой славе
Я хотел прожить пропащим.

Я хотел, чтоб сердце глуше
Вспоминало сад и лето,
Где под музыку лягушек
Я растил себя поэтом.

Там теперь такая ж осень…
Клён и липы, в окна комнат
Ветки лапами забросив,
Ищут тех, которых помнят.

Их давно уж нет на свете.
Месяц на простом погосте
На крестах лучами метит,
Что и мы придём к ним в гости.

"Darling, come, let's sit together...", 1923

Darling, come, let's sit together,
Gazing gently at each other.
May I, under your soft stare,
Lose myself in sensous blizzard.

Your lush locks, almost albescent,
The appeasing golden autumn -
All this was a kind of godsend
For the hopeless, troubled heartthrob.

Long ago I left my homeland,
Where meadows bloom and thickets.
Full of urban, bitter glory,
I was to become a trinket.

Yet my heart beats even stronger
Thinking of my sun-soaked homestead,
Where, to the songs of froglets,
I was growing up a poet.

There now is also autumn…
Through the windows, always open,
Maple branches reach deep into,
Seeking their unforgotten.

Yet they are no longer there.
New moon, over at the churchyard,
Marks the crosses with its white rays,
As if saying we're awaited.

Что и мы, отжив тревоги,
Перейдём под эти кущи.
Все волнистые дороги
Только радость льют живущим.

Дорогая, сядь же рядом,
Поглядим в глаза друг другу.
Я хочу под кротким взглядом
Слушать чувственную вьюгу.

As if saying we will also
Come to rest there, freed from worries.
All life's winding, thorny roads
Give the living only jollies.

So please come, let's sit together,
Gazing gently at each other.
I want, under your soft stare,
To be caught in sensuous blizzard.

"Мне грустно на тебя смотреть…", 1923

Мне грустно на тебя смотреть,
Какая боль, какая жалость!
Знать, только ивовая медь
Нам в сентябре с тобой осталась.

Чужие губы разнесли
Твоё тепло и трепет тела.
Как будто дождик моросит
С души, немного омертвелой.

Ну что ж! Я не боюсь его.
Иная радость мне открылась.
Ведь не осталось ничего,
Как только жёлтый тлен и сырость.

Ведь и себя я не сберёг
Для тихой жизни, для улыбок.
Так мало пройдено дорог,
Так много сделано ошибок.

Смешная жизнь, смешной разлад.
Так было и так будет после.
Как кладбище, усеян сад
В берёз изглоданные кости.

Вот так же отцветём и мы
И отшумим, как гости сада…
Коль нет цветов среди зимы,
Так и грустить о них не надо.

"It saddens me to look at you…", 1923

It saddens me to look at you,
Oh, what a pain, and what a sorrow!
September knows that we are through,
So left us with this willow copper.

The alien lips have kissed away
Your body's warmth, your gentle quiver.
It is as if a drizzling rain
Patted my soggy soul, once-living.

Oh, well! Of it I'm not afraid.
For I have found a different pleasance.
For nothing's left for me except
The yellow dust and greyish dampness.

Indeed, I never saved myself
For peaceful living, and for smiles.
I've made a hell lot of mistakes
While treading down just one pathway.

A funny life, a funny rift.
It's always been like that and will be.
Like graveyard, our garden keeps
Exhausted bones of tired birch trees.

A day will come, and we'll too die,
And be a garden, ever dormant…
If there's no bloom in wintertime,
Then there's no need for us to mourn it.

"Мне осталась одна забава…", 1923

Мне осталась одна забава:
Пальцы в рот — и веселый свист.
Прокатилась дурная слава,
Что похабник я и скандалист.

Ах! Какая смешная потеря!
Много в жизни смешных потерь.
Стыдно мне, что я в бога верил.
Горько мне, что не верю теперь.

Золотые, далёкие дали!
Все сжигает житейская мреть.
И похабничал я и скандалил
Для того, чтобы ярче гореть.

Дар поэта — ласкать и карябать,
Роковая на нём печать.
Розу белую с черною жабой
Я хотел на земле повенчать.

Пусть не сладились, пусть не сбылись
Эти помыслы розовых дней.
Но коль черти в душе гнездились —
Значит, ангелы жили в ней.
Вот за это веселие мути,
Отправляясь с ней в край иной,
Я хочу при последней минуте
Попросить тех, кто будет со мной, —
Чтоб за все за грехи мои тяжкие,
За неверие в благодать
Положили меня в русской рубашке
Под иконами умирать.

"I am left wit but one entertainment…", 1923

I am left with but one entertainment:
Hand to lips – and whistling away.
It's been rumoured that I'm a debaser,
Who rampages day after day.

Such a funny and silly attrition!
Life is full of setbacks of the kind.
Shame on me I was never religious.
Sad I still don't believe in God now.

Unattainable, golden distance!
Life is known to make everything trite.
Yes, I've been a foul-mouth and a hardcase -
Just to be a more powerful sight.

Poets' gift is to scar and to cuddle,
There's inside them a fatal code.
As for me, I came here to couple
A white rose with an ugly black toad.

So they failed to reach an agreement,
Those intentions of my golden youth.
But if my soul was haunted by demons –
Angels must have once dwelled there, too.
Overcome with this drunken riot,
At the edge of another world,
I would like to address my crowd,
Who, I hope, will be there when I go.
For the terrible sins I've committed,
For distrusting Divine in my life -
Lay me, dressed in a national garment,
Under Russian church icons - to die.

"Ты такая ж простая, как все…", 1923

Ты такая ж простая, как все,
Как сто тысяч других в России.
Знаешь ты одинокий рассвет,
Знаешь холод осени синий.

По-смешному я сердцем влип,
Я по-глупому мысли занял.
Твой иконный и строгий лик
По часовням висел в рязанях.

Я на эти иконы плевал,
Чтил я грубость и крик в повесе,
А теперь вдруг растут слова
Самых нежных и кротких песен.

Не хочу я лететь в зенит,
Слишком многое телу надо.
Что ж так имя твое звенит,
Словно августовская прохлада?

Я не нищий, ни жалок, ни мал
И умею расслышать за пылом:
С детства нравиться я понимал
Кобелям да степным кобылам.
Потому и себя не сберег
Для тебя, для нее и для этой.
Невеселого счастья залог —
Сумасшедшее сердце поэта.
Потому и грущу, осев,
Словно в листья, в глаза косые…
Ты такая ж простая, как все,
Как сто тысяч других в России.

"But you are just like everyone else...", 1923

But you are just like everyone else,
Like a million others in Russia.
You are used to the lonely sunrise,
And the blue chill of autumn rustle.

Silly heart got me into this mess,
Idle mind needed something to grapple.
Your church icon-like, rigid face
Could adorn our village chapels.

In the past I would spit at those 'boards',
Sheer rudeness and bawl I worshipped.
Now I found myself full of words
For the songs most benign and devoted.

I'm not willing to give myself in,
Pampering my insatiable body.
Yet your name keeps vibrating in me,
Like the heaven-sent freshness of August.

I'm not poor nor ugly nor short,
And can hear another's prayers:
As a kid, I was always adored
By stud-dogs and worn-out steppe mares.
But, alas, I can't bear a part
In your life or in hers or another's.
Poet's crazy and thoughtless heart
Can bring nothing but chagrin and troubles.
That is why I can't help feeling sad,
Giving way to this chilly, blue rustle...
For you are just like everyone else,
Like a million others in Russia.

"Ты прохладой меня не мучай...", 1923

Ты прохладой меня не мучай
И не спрашивай, сколько мне лет,
Одержимый тяжелой падучей,
Я душой стал, как жёлтый скелет.

Было время, когда из предместья
Я мечтал по-мальчишески — в дым,
Что я буду богат и известен
И что всеми я буду любим.

Да! Богат я, богат с излишком.
Был цилиндр, а теперь его нет.
Лишь осталась одна манишка
С модной парой избитых штиблет.

И известность моя не хуже, —
От Москвы по парижскую рвань
Мое имя наводит ужас,
Как заборная, громкая брань.

И любовь, не забавное ль дело?
Ты целуешь, а губы как жесть.
Знаю, чувство мое перезрело,
А твоё не сумеет расцвесть.

Мне пока горевать еще рано,
Ну, а если есть грусть — не беда!
Золотей твоих кос по курганам
Молодая шумит лебеда.

"Don't torment me with cold demeanour...", 1923

Don't torment me with cold demeanour
And don't ask me how old I am.
Overcome with the falling evil,
My soul stripped to a skeleton frame.

In the old days, a village child,
I was dreaming - beyond any hope,
That one day I'd be rich and renowned,
And that I'd be revered by all.

Well! I *am* rich, for my own liking.
My one top hat I managed to lose.
All I've left is a single dicky,
And a pair of trendy, worn boots.

My publicity is just as good as -
From Muscovy to Paris crooks,
My name seems to insult the senses,
Like the loudest, vulgar abuse.

And our love, isn't it just as funny?
When you kiss me, your lips feel so cold.
For my feeling is now over ripen,
As for yours, it will never burst forth.

It's too early for me to shed tears,
But if I do get sad – no big deal!
Even brighter than your golden tresses,
Young fat-hen blooms in burial hills.

Я хотел бы опять в ту местность,
Чтоб под шум молодой лебеды
Утонуть навсегда в неизвестность
И мечтать по-мальчишески — в дым.

Но мечтать о другом, о новом,
Непонятном земле и траве,
Что не выразить сердцу словом,
И не знает назвать человек.

I would like to return to that region
Where, lost on the fat-hen slopes,
I could sink into endless oblivion
And dream on, like a child - beyond hope.

But dream on about things new and different,
Inexplicit for land and for grass.
About something so sacred, so secret
That can't name our human hearts.

"Я усталым таким ещё не был…", 1923

Я усталым таким ещё не был.
В эту серую морозь и слизь
Мне приснилось рязанское небо
И моя непутёвая жизнь.

Много женщин меня любило,
Да и сам я любил не одну,
Не от этого ль тёмная сила
Приучила меня к вину.

Бесконечные пьяные ночи
И в разгуле тоска не впервь!
Не с того ли глаза мне точит,
Словно синие листья червь?

Не больна мне ничья измена,
И не радует лёгкость побед,—
Тех волос золотое сено
Превращается в серый цвет.

Превращаются в пепел и воды,
Когда цедит осенняя муть.
Мне не жаль вас, прошедшие годы,—
Ничего не хочу вернуть.

Я устал себя мучить без цели,
И с улыбкою странной лица
Полюбил я носить в лёгком теле
Тихий свет и покой мертвеца…

"It's the first time I've been so exhausted...", 1923

It's the first time I've been so exhausted.
In this weather of grey, chilly slime,
I was dreaming about my homeland,
And my useless and troubled life.

Countless women have called me 'beloved',
Countless women I've called that myself,
Maybe that's why the wicked power
Got me hooked on wine and affray.

Endless nights spent in drunken partying,
Mixed with onsets of pain and grief!
Maybe that's why my eyes look so empty,
Like some worm-eaten, bluish leaves.

When I'm cheated on, I just don't care,
And I'm not into easy prey -
Golden hay of my once swanky hair
Has dried out and turned mucky grey.

My past turned into ashes and water,
Tainted with this autumnal slack.
Years gone by, I don't pity you, sorry, -
There is nothing that I would want back.

I am tired of this aimless torment,
And suppressing a weird smile,
I like feeling a bit like a dead man,
Full of solace and quiet shine.

И теперь даже стало не тяжко
Ковылять из притона в притон,
Как в смирительную рубашку,
Мы природу берём в бетон.

И во мне, вот по тем же законам,
Умиряется бешеный пыл.
Но и всё ж отношусь я с поклоном
К тем полям, что когда-то любил.

В те края, где я рос под клёном,
Где резвился на жёлтой траве,—
Шлю привет воробьям и воронам,
И рыдающей в ночь сове.

Я кричу им в весенние дали:
«Птицы милые, в синюю дрожь
Передайте, что я отскандалил,—
Пусть хоть ветер теперь начинает
Под микитки дубасить рожь».

It no longer feels bad to be trudging
From one den to another den.
As if in a confinement jacket,
We array nature in cement.

And in me, for the same weird reason,
Dies down slowly the wild blaze.
Yet I still care for and revere
Those plough fields where I spent my best days.

Oh, those meads full of old maples,
Where I basked in the yellow grass, -
Send my love to the crows, and the sparrows,
And the owl that weeps at dusk.

I am calling to them from the offing:
'Birdies, dear, it's me, would you please
Tell the blue chill that I am done brawling, -
May the wind now turn vicious and storming,
Punching rye fields below the ribs.'

"Этой грусти теперь не рассыпать...", 1924

Этой грусти теперь не рассыпать
Звонким смехом далёких лет.
Отцвела моя белая липа,
Отзвенел соловьиный рассвет.

Для меня было всё тогда новым,
Много в сердце теснилось чувств,
А теперь даже нежное слово
Горьким плодом срывается с уст.
И знакомые взору просторы
Уж не так под луной хороши.
Буераки... пеньки... косогоры
Обпечалили русскую ширь.

Нездоровое, хилое, низкое,
Водянистая, серая гладь.
Это всё мне родное и близкое,
От чего так легко зарыдать.

Покосившаяся избенка,
Плач овцы, и вдали на ветру
Машет тощим хвостом лошадёнка,
Заглядевшись в неласковый пруд.
Это всё, что зовем мы родиной,
Это всё, отчего на ней
Пьют и плачут в одно с непогодиной,
Дожидаясь улыбчивых дней.
Потому никому не рассыпать
Эту грусть смехом ранних лет.
Отцвела моя белая липа,
Отзвенел соловьиный рассвет.

"Nowadays I can't scatter this sadness…", 1924

Nowadays I can't scatter this sadness
With the laughter of distant years.
My beautiful linden has faded,
Done and dusted are summer daybreaks.

All for me was then like for the first time.
In my heart, many feelings pressed through.
But today, even delicate white lies
Fall from lips like some rotten fruit.
And the landscape akin to my glance
Is no longer so nice in the night.
For the hillsides, ditches, and stumps
Have spoiled the pretty sight.

All around is unhealthy and low.
A watery, greyish bog place.
Yet the sight is so native and close,
And always brings tears to my face.

A rickety, small country home.
The weeping of sheep and there, far away,
Waves her tail a skinny horse,
Staring at a cloudy lake.
This is all that we call Motherland.
This is everything why in it
People cry and drink every other day,
Awaiting a better fate.
That is why I can't scatter this sadness
With the laughter of early years.
What a pity – my linden has faded,
Gone for good are the summer daybreaks.

"Воспоминание", 1924

Теперь октябрь не тот,
Не тот октябрь теперь.
В стране, где свищет непогода,
Ревел и выл
Октябрь, как зверь,
Октябрь семнадцатого года.
Я помню жуткий
Снежный день.
Его я видел мутным взглядом.
Железная витала тень
Над омраченным Петроградом».
Уже все чуяли грозу,
Уже все знали что-то,
Знали,
Что не напрасно, знать, везут
Солдаты черепах из стали.
Рассыпались...
Уселись в ряд...
У публики дрожат поджилки...
И кто-то вдруг сорвал плакат
Со стен трусливой учредилки.
И началось... Взметнулись взоры,
Войной гражданскою горя,
И дымом пламенной «Авроры»
Взошла железная заря.
Свершилась участь роковая,
И над страной под вопли «матов»
Взметнулась надпись огневая:
"Совет Рабочих Депутатов".

"A Memory", 1924

October's different now,
It's not the same October.
Across the Russian plains,
The tempest had been roaring
And howling, like a wounded beast.
October 1917.
I keep in mind a dismal
Snowy day.
I saw it blearily.
An iron mist had hung, like shade,
Over the gloomy city.
We all could scent a threat.
We knew something was coming.
It must have been the reason why,
Like giant turtles, crawled along
Columns of armour.
Came to a halt…
Took up positions…
The crowd braced themselves…
Then hell broke loose, it all began
With launching an offensive.
And people ran… and rushed about.
Eyes full of pain, ready to mourn.
And then «Aurora» cruiser fired,
And ushered in the iron dawn.
The fatal dice of death were rolled,
And shouting obscenities,
The country waved a blood-stained banner:
"Soviet of Workers' Deputies***".

*** A civil body representing five trade unions and 96 factories from
around St Petersburg, which was radicalised in the course of the
October Revolution.

"Мы теперь уходим понемногу…", 1924

Мы теперь уходим понемногу
В ту страну, где тишь и благодать.
Может быть, и скоро мне в дорогу
Бренные пожитки собирать.

Милые березовые чащи!
Ты, земля! И вы, равнин пески!
Перед этим сонмом уходящих
Я не в силах скрыть моей тоски.

Слишком я любил на этом свете
Всё, что душу облекает в плоть.
Мир осинам, что, раскинув ветви,
Загляделись в розовую водь!

Много дум я в тишине продумал,
Много песен про себя сложил,
И на этой на земле угрюмой
Счастлив тем, что я дышал и жил.

Счастлив тем, что целовал я женщин,
Мял цветы, валялся на траве
И зверьё, как братьев наших меньших,
Никогда не бил по голове.
Знаю я, что не цветут там чащи,
Не звенит лебяжьей шеей рожь.
Оттого пред сонмом уходящих
Я всегда испытываю дрожь.
Знаю я, что в той стране не будет
Этих нив, златящихся во мгле…
Оттого и дороги мне люди,
Что живут со мною на земле.

"Day by day we're gradually departing...", 1924

Day by day we're gradually departing
For that land where peace prevails, and bliss.
Maybe it is time I also started
Packing up my scanty, worldly things.

Oh, my dear, lovely birch tree brushwood!
My beloved land! The flatland sands!
Watching this departing, hazy crowd,
I just can't help feeling mighty sad.

I've been too attached to all things frail,
Putting fleshly lusts before my soul.
Peace be with the aspen trees forever,
As they watch the rosy water flow!

Still I've done a lot of silent thinking.
I've chastised and praised myself to bits.
Given that this world is not a picnic,
I am happy to have lived and breathed.

I am happy I've been kissing women,
Smelling flowers, rolling on the grass.
But above all, I have always treated
Every animal as one of us.
And I know - *that land* has no green brushwood,
And its rye fields stale without a breeze.
That's why watching this departing crowd,
I can't help but buckle at the knees.
In that land, there won't be any meadows,
Set aflame with golden light at night...
That's why I have learnt to love and treasure
Every single person in my life.

"Письмо матери", 1924

Ты жива еще, моя старушка?
Жив и я. Привет тебе, привет!
Пусть струится над твоей избушкой
Тот вечерний несказанный свет.

Пишут мне, что ты, тая тревогу,
Загрустила шибко обо мне,
Что ты часто ходишь на дорогу
В старомодном ветхом шушуне.

И тебе в вечернем синем мраке
Часто видится одно и то ж:
Будто кто-то мне в кабацкой драке
Саданул под сердце финский нож.

Ничего, родная! Успокойся.
Это только тягостная бредь.
Не такой уж горький я пропойца,
Чтоб, тебя не видя, умереть.

Я по-прежнему такой же нежный
И мечтаю только лишь о том,
Чтоб скорее от тоски мятежной
Воротиться в низенький наш дом.

Я вернусь, когда раскинет ветви
По-весеннему наш белый сад.
Только ты меня уж на рассвете
Не буди, как восемь лет назад.

"Letter to Mother", 1924

You alive and well, my dear mother?
So am I, and sending you my love.
May it always shine above your house,
That heart-warming, vespertinal glow.

I am told that you are getting worried
And that you are missing me a lot.
That you're coming out on the road
In your shabby and old-fashioned coat.

That at night, the same disturbing image
Often comes to haunt your mental sight:
And you see me getting badly injured
In a random, drunken tavern fight.

Don't you worry much, my dear mother.
That is nothing more than a bad dream.
I have not yet turned a hopeless drunkard -
Promise I won't die till you see me.

I am still your loving little boyo
And am dreaming still of nothing more
Than to flee this deep, insurgent sorrow
By returning to our humble home.

I'll be back when our luscious garden
Blooms all white in marvellous spring glow.
Only, please, don't wake me up at sunrise,
Like you did those eight summers ago.

Не буди того, что отмечталось,
Не волнуй того, что не сбылось.
Слишком раннюю утрату и усталость
Испытать мне в жизни привелось.

И молиться не учи меня. Не надо!
К старому возврата больше нет.
Ты одна мне помощь и отрада,
Ты одна мне несказанный свет.

Так забудь же про свою тревогу,
Не грусти так шибко обо мне.
Не ходи так часто на дорогу
В старомодном ветхом шушуне.

Don't wake up the dreams that never happened,
Don't upset what failed to hold up.
For in my life, I have had too many
Early losses, frazzles and breakups.

And don't try to teach me all those prayers!
There's no coming back to olden times.
You're my only help and consolation,
My heart-warming, vespertinal light.

So forget, my darling, all your worries,
And – I pray - don't miss your son a lot.
Don't come out so often on the road
In your shabby and old-fashioned coat.

Отговорила роща золотая
Берёзовым, весёлым языком,
И журавли, печально пролетая,
Уж не жалеют больше ни о ком.

Кого жалеть? Ведь каждый в мире странник.
Пройдет, зайдет и вновь оставит дом.
О всех ушедших грезит коноплянник
С широким месяцем над голубым прудом.

Стою один среди равнины голой,
А журавлей относит ветер в даль,
Я полон дум о юности весёлой,
Но ничего в прошедшем мне не жаль.

Не жаль мне лет, растраченных напрасно,
Не жаль души сиреневую цветь.
В саду горит костер рябины красной,
Но никого не может он согреть.

Не обгорят рябиновые кисти,
От желтизны не пропадет трава.
Как дерево роняет тихо листья,
Так я роняю грустные слова.

И если время, ветром разметая,
Сгребет их все в один ненужный ком.
Скажите так... что роща золотая
Отговорила милым языком.

"The golden birch grove suddenly went quiet...",
1924

The golden birch grove suddenly went quiet:
Its merry rustle is no longer heard.
Over the grove, a flock of cranes is flying,
Weeping for no one anymore.

Who to lament for? Everyone's a rover.
We come and go and then come back again.
Hemp fields and moon above the blue backwater
Will grieve for all those gone-without-end.

Standing alone amidst the barren low land,
Watching the pensive cranes drifting away.
I'm full of thoughts about my merry boyhood,
And yet I don't regret my yesterdays.

I don't regret the years that have been buried,
I don't regret the faded bloom of youth.
The garden is aflame with rowanberries,
But this bonfire's cold and of no use.

This flame will never char the rowan trusses,
Nor will it make the grass beneath them scorched.
Like tired, silent trees that shed their tassels,
I shed my quiet and dejected words.

And should the wind of time descend upon them,
And blow them all into a needless heap,
You may just say... it is the golden birch grove
That once was merry but is now asleep.

"Ах, как много на свете кошек…"
Сестре Шуре, 1925

Ах, как много на свете кошек,
Нам с тобой их не счесть никогда.
Сердцу снится душистый горошек,
И звенит голубая звезда.

Наяву ли, в бреду иль спросонок,
Только помню с далёкого дня —
На лежанке мурлыкал котёнок,
Безразлично смотря на меня.

Я ещё тогда был ребёнок,
Но под бабкину песню вскок
Он бросался, как юный тигрёнок,
На оброненный ею клубок.

Всё прошло. Потерял я бабку,
А ещё через несколько лет
Из кота того сделали шапку,
А её износил наш дед.

"Oh, there're so many cats out there…"
To sister Shura, 1925

Oh, there're so many out there,
Bit too many to treasure, alas.
In my dreams, I can see sweet peas growing,
And can hear the jingling of stars.

Was it real or was I light-headed,
Only this I remember quite well –
A small kitten was eyeing me strangely
While gently purring away.

I was then only a toddler,
Who liked watching granny at work,
And the kitten, much like a small tiger,
Would be clawing the yarn she would drop.

Time had passed, and so did the granny,
And a couple of years after that,
The kitten became a fur hat
That was then worn away by granddad.

"Вечером синим, вечером лунным...", 1925

Вечером синим, вечером лунным
Был я когда-то красивым и юным.

Неудержимо, неповторимо
Всё пролетело... далече... мимо...

Сердце остыло, и выцвели очи...
Синее счастье! Лунные ночи!

'On a blue night, such moonlit night...', 1925

On a blue night, such moonlit night,
I was once handsome, I was once young.

So uncontained, one of a kind.
And it's all over... out of sight...

Heart made of ice, colourless eyes...
Oh, my lost happiness! Oh, moonlit nights!

"Снежная равнина, белая луна…", 1925

Снежная равнина, белая луна,
Саваном покрыта наша сторона.
И берёзы в белом плачут по лесам.
Кто погиб здесь? Умер? Уж не я ли сам ?

"White snow, like a shroud, covered our plains...",
1925

White snow, like a shroud, covered our plains,
Eerie moon looks down over its domains.
And the mournful birch trees hold their white vigil.
Who has died here? Perished? Oh, could this be me?

"Ты меня не любишь, не жалеешь...", 1925

Ты меня не любишь, не жалеешь,
Разве я немного не красив?
Не смотря в лицо, от страсти млеешь,
Мне на плечи руки опустив.

Молодая, с чувственным оскалом,
Я с тобой не нежен и не груб.
Расскажи мне, скольких ты ласкала?
Сколько рук ты помнишь? Сколько губ?

Знаю я — они прошли, как тени,
Не коснувшись твоего огня,
Многим ты садилась на колени,
А теперь сидишь вот у меня.

Пусть твои полузакрыты очи
И ты думаешь о ком-нибудь другом,
Я ведь сам люблю тебя не очень,
Утопая в дальнем, дорогом.

Этот пыл не называй судьбою,
Легкодумна вспыльчивая связь,
— Как случайно встретился с тобою,
Улыбнусь, спокойно разойдясь.

Да и ты пойдёшь своей дорогой
Распылять безрадостные дни,
Только нецелованных не трогай,
Только негоревших не мани.

"You don't love me, nor do you have pity...", 1925

You don't love me, nor do you have pity,
　　Is it that I'm not handsome enough?
Hiding head, yet acting like a sweetheart,
　　Don't you worry - I won't call your bluff.

You're so young and pretty, and so fleshly,
　　Which I neither like in you nor hate.
Am I just another fleeting passion
　　In the maze of countless lips and hands?

So, I guess they are now only shadows,
Who could never touch your shielded heart,
Many men have called you their treasure,
　　I will do so too, at least for now.

I don't mind your gaze being quite vacant,
Like you're really somewhere else tonight.
I'm myself elsewhere, for that matter.
　　Overcome with longing for the past.

Don't mistake this passion for a karma,
Passions are so thoughtless and short-lived,
　　– Let's part casually, without drama,
After all, it's how we chanced to meet.

And along you'll go, young and unburdened,
　　Wearing away your joyless days,
Just leave out those who are still verdant,
Save them from the all-consuming blaze.

И когда с другим по переулку
Ты пройдёшь, болтая про любовь,
Может быть, я выйду на прогулку,
И с тобою встретимся мы вновь.

Отвернув к другому ближе плечи
И немного наклонившись вниз,
Ты мне скажешь тихо: «Добрый вечер!»
Я отвечу: «Добры вечер, miss».

И ничто души не потревожит,
И ничто её не бросит в дрожь, —
Кто любил, уж тот любить не может,
Кто сгорел, того не подожжёшь.

One day we will meet again, no doubt,
A sarcastic gesture from above,
You will walk with someone in the crowd,
Chatting happily about love.

With your back to me, your voice unmeaning,
As if overlooking an abyss,
You will whisper quietly: «Good evening!»
I will glance at you and say: «Night, miss».

I am safe now from life's endless cheating,
Nothing now can get under my skin, –
He who loved for real, shall not repeat it,
He who's dead, shall not be dead again.

"В этом мире я только прохожий...", 1925

В этом мире я только прохожий,
Ты махни мне весёлой рукой.
У осеннего месяца тоже
Свет ласкающий, тихий такой.

В первый раз я от месяца греюсь,
В первый раз от прохлады согрет,
И опять и живу, и надеюсь
На любовь, которой уж нет.

Это сделала наша равнинность,
Посолённая белью песка,
И измятая чья-то невинность,
И кому-то родная тоска.

Потому и навеки не скрою,
Что любить не отдельно, не врозь —
Нам одною любовью с тобою
Эту родину привелось.

"In this world I'm an idle walker...", 1925

In this world I'm an idle walker,
Wave to me as I pass you by.
Did you know - a new moon in autumn
Has that soothing and quiet shine.

For the first time I bask in the moon glow,
For the first time its chill made me warm.
Once again I'm alive and look forward
To the love that is no more.

We're of one blood with Russian flatland,
With its white bitter-salty expanse,
Where we all have experienced plenty
Of lost innocence and despair.

That is why we are bound forever,
Hand in hand and never apart,
To be feeling that bond with our homeland
And to love it no matter what.

"Какая ночь! Я не могу…", 1925

Какая ночь! Я не могу.
Не спится мне. Такая лунность.
Еще как будто берегу
В душе утраченную юность.

Подруга охладевших лет,
Не называй игру любовью,
Пусть лучше этот лунный свет
Ко мне струится к изголовью.
Пусть искаженные черты
Он обрисовывает смело, —
Ведь разлюбить не сможешь ты,
Как полюбить ты не сумела.

Любить лишь можно только раз.
Вот оттого ты мне чужая,
Что липы тщетно манят нас,
В сугробы ноги погружая.

Ведь знаю я и знаешь ты,
Что в этот отсвет лунный, синий
На этих липах не цветы —
На этих липах снег да иней.
Что отлюбили мы давно,
Ты не меня, а я — другую,
И нам обоим все равно
Играть в любовь недорогую.
Но все ж ласкай и обнимай
В лукавой страсти поцелуя,
Пусть сердцу вечно снится май
И та, что навсегда люблю я.

"Oh, what a night! I cannot sleep...", 1925

Oh, what a night! I cannot sleep.
Who could – the moon as bright as fire.
It is as if I treasured still
Inside my soul, my long-lost springtime.

My girlfriend of the days grown cold,
Don't call this game a real something.
Just let this eerie moon glow
Glide through the window to my bedside.
Let moonlight in, let it roam free,
Flashing my features, now distorted.
I know - you can't stop loving me,
Because you never really started.

Love only happens to us once.
That's why to me you are stranger.
The linden trees won't beckon us,
Embedded deep in frosty snow banks.

For I know well, and you do, too,
That in this sapphirine, rich moon glow
The linden trees are not in bloom,
The linden trees are dressed in white snow.
We're long past loving now, alas.
And we have never loved *each other*.
That's why it really makes no sense
Pretending that this fling means something.
Yet – pray – caress and fondle me
With kisses full of cunning fervour.
May my heart always dream of spring,
And her, who I will love forever.

"Мой путь", 1925

Жизнь входит в берега.
Села давнишний житель,
Я вспоминаю то,
Что видел я в краю.
Стихи мои,
Спокойно расскажите
Про жизнь мою.
Изба крестьянская.
Хомутный запах дегтя,
Божница старая,
Лампады кроткий свет.
Как хорошо,
Что я сберёг те
Все ощущенья детских лет.
Под окнами
Костёр метели белой.
Мне девять лет.
Лежанка, бабка, кот…
И бабка что-то грустное,
Степное пела,
Порой зевая
И крестя свой рот.
Метель ревела.
Под оконцем
Как будто бы плясали мертвецы.
Тогда империя
Вела войну с японцем,
И всем далекие
Мерещились кресты.
Тогда не знал я
Чёрных дел России.
Не знал, зачем и почему война.

"My life", 1925

Life's settling down at last.
The old-established villager,
I reminisce about the things
I used to see and like.
My poems,
Tell a composed story
About my life.
A peasant's cottage.
A distinct tar scent,
The ancient icon-case,
The icon-lamp's soft glow.
I feel so blessed
To have preserved that,
All that I'd lived on as a boy.
Outside -
The snowstorm's white campfire.
I'm nine years old.
The stove-couch, granny, cat…
My granny hummed a song
That almost had me crying,
Although she'd often stop
And yawn, or cross herself.
The snowstorm raged.
Below the window,
I could make out ghostly shapes.
The country then
Had been at war with Nippon,
So everywhere one looked, one saw just crapes.
I knew not then
Of Russia's twisted plotting.
What for and why
There had been war.

Рязанские поля,
Где мужики косили,
Где сеяли свой хлеб,
Была моя страна.
Я помню только то,
Что мужики роптали,
Бранились в чёрта,
В Бога и в царя.
Но им в ответ
Лишь улыбались дали
Да наша жидкая
Лимонная заря.
Тогда впервые
С рифмой я схлестнулся.
От сонма чувств
Вскружилась голова.
И я сказал:
Коль этот зуд проснулся,
Всю душу выплещу в слова.
Года далёкие,
Теперь вы, как в тумане.
И помню, дед мне
С грустью говорил:
«Пустое дело…
Ну, а если тянет —
Пиши про рожь,
Но больше про кобыл».
Тогда в мозгу,
Влеченьем к музе сжатом,
Текли мечтанья
В тайной тишине,
Что буду я
Известным и богатым
И будет памятник стоять в Рязани мне.

Our Ryazan fields
Where peasants had been mowing
And sowing their crops
Was what I'd called my home.
I just recall them moan
And growl in defiance,
Cursing the deuce,
The Tsar, and even God.
But in reply,
The distance only smiled,
And grinned our slushy,
Lemon-yellow dawn.
Then for the first time
I tried versifying.
A host of feelings
Gave me a head rush.
And so I thought:
Since that pursuit has found me,
I'll splash my heart and soul into rhymes.
Those distant years,
As in a fog, are blurry.
But I recall my granddad
Who would say:
'A pointless whim…
This useless writing hobby -
But if you must,
Write about rye, or mares rather, hey'.
In my mind then,
Obsessed with writing passion,
I cherished rosy,
Silent, sacred dreams
That one day
I'd be rich and famous
And have a statue in Ryazan – all to myself.

В пятнадцать лет
Взлюбил я до печенок
И сладко думал,
Лишь уединюсь,
Что я на этой
Лучшей из девчонок,
Достигнув возраста, женюсь.
. . . .
Года текли.
Года меняют лица —
Другой на них
Ложится свет.
Мечтатель сельский —
Я в столице
Стал первокласснейший поэт.
И, заболев
Писательскою скукой,
Пошел скитаться я
Средь разных стран,
Не веря встречам,
Не томясь разлукой,
Считая мир весь за обман.
Тогда я понял,
Что такое Русь.
Я понял, что такое слава.
И потому мне
В душу грусть
Вошла, как горькая отрава.
На кой мне черт,
Что я поэт!..
И без меня в достатке дряни.
Пускай я сдохну,
Только…
Нет, не ставьте памятник в Рязани!

Then, aged fifteen,
I fell in love quite madly,
And thought with pleasure -
Once I fly the nest,
I'll ask that girlie,
Finest out there,
When both are old enough, to make my match.
. . . .
Years glided past.
Years change our faces –
Making them strange,
As if makeshift.
A village dreamer,
I went places,
Selling to all my first class gift.
And getting sick
With prickly writing dullness,
I wandered off to rove
In every land,
Ignoring feelings,
Breaking up with gusto,
Believing life to be a sham.
I understood then
What my country was.
And fame to me became all clear.
That's why deep grief
Engulfed my soul,
Turning to flood my every tear.
Well, I'm a goddam poet,
So?...
There's just enough of scum already.
May I be cursed and die,
But...
No, I want no statue in my homeland!

Россия… Царщина…
Тоска…
И снисходительность дворянства.
Ну что ж!
Так принимай, Москва,
Отчаянное хулиганство.
Посмотрим —
Кто кого возьмёт!
И вот в стихах моих
Забила
В салонный вылощенный
Сброд
Мочой рязанская кобыла.
Не нравится?
Да, вы правы —
Привычка к Лориган
И к розам…
Но этот хлеб,
Что жрёте вы,—
Ведь мы его того-с…
Навозом…
. . . .
Ещё прошли года.
В годах такое было,
О чём в словах
Всего не рассказать:
На смену царщине
С величественной силой
Рабочая предстала рать.
Устав таскаться
По чужим пределам,
Вернулся я
В родимый дом.
Зеленокосая, в юбчонке белой

Rossiya… Tsardom…
The snore-fest…
And upper class's condescendence.
Well then, sweet Moskva,
Brace yourself
For reckless tantrums of a badass.
We'll see –
Who gets to win hands down!
And suddenly
My verse bespattered
That fancy-looking boring
Crowd
With urine of a Ryazan mare.
Not keen on that?
Yes, you are right –
I get your noble tastes,
For sure…
But this white bread
That you so like –
Comes from the soil…
Rich in manure…

. . . .

More years went swiftly by,
Beholding things so queer
That mere words
Cannot communicate:
Replacing Tsardom,
With its stately vigour,
The workers' army came on stage.
Tired of roving
In the foreign bounds,
I made back to
Ancestral land.
Green-plaited, wearing a white dress,

Стоит береза над прудом.
Уж и береза!
Чудная… А груди…
Таких грудей
У женщин не найдёшь.
С полей обрызганные солнцем
Люди
Везут навстречу мне
В телегах рожь.
Им не узнать меня,
Я им прохожий.
Но вот проходит
Баба, не взглянув.
Какой-то ток
Невыразимой дрожи
Я чувствую во всю спину.
Ужель она?
Ужели не узнала?
Ну и пускай,
Пускай себе пройдёт…
И без меня ей
Горечи немало —
Недаром лёг
Страдальчески так рот.
По вечерам,
Надвинув ниже кепи,
Чтобы не выдать
Холода очей,—
Хожу смотреть я
Скошенные степи
И слушать,
Как звенит ручей.

A birch tree stands over the lake.
Look at that beauty!
And her lovely nipples…
Not every girl
Could boast a set that fine.
Back from the fields,
Sun-treated men and women
Bring carts and wagons
Full of rye.
Not recognizing me,
I'm just a stranger.
But there goes one woman,
Her head down.
As if a flow
Of some unknown trembling
Has passed right down my rigid spine.
Could it be she?
Could she not recognise me?
Oh well, let her
Be on her way…
Without me
She's had enough of grieving –
It's not for nothing
That her face is grey.
Night after night,
Pulling my cap right down,
Not to betray the coldness
Of my eyes, -
I wander out
Into the mowed grassland
To meditate on field brooks
Chiming by.

Ну что же?
Молодость прошла!
Пора приняться мне
За дело,
Чтоб озорливая душа
Уже по-зрелому запела.
И пусть иная жизнь села
Меня наполнит
Новой силой,
Как раньше
К славе привела
Родная русская кобыла.

Well then?
Alas, I'm young no more!
Time I got down
To business,
So that my playful, naughty soul
Could tune into mature singing.
May this another, village life
Fill me with vigour
Ever-present,
The way
I once got recognised
For writing about Russian mares.

"Чёрный человек", 1923- 25

Друг мой, друг мой,
Я очень и очень болен.
Сам не знаю, откуда взялась эта боль.
То ли ветер свистит
Над пустым и безлюдным полем,
То ль, как рощу в сентябрь,
Осыпает мозги алкоголь.
Голова моя машет ушами,
Как крыльями птица.
Ей на шее ноги
Маячить больше невмочь.
Чёрный человек,
Чёрный, чёрный,
Чёрный человек
На кровать ко мне садится,
Чёрный человек
Спать не даёт мне всю ночь.
Чёрный человек
Водит пальцем по мерзкой книге
И, гнусавя надо мной,
Как над усопшим монах,
Читает мне жизнь
Какого-то прохвоста и забулдыги,
Нагоняя на душу тоску и страх.
Чёрный, человек
Чёрный, чёрный...
«Слушай, слушай, —
Бормочет он мне, —
В книге много прекраснейших
Мыслей и планов.
Этот человек проживал в стране

"The Dark Man", 1923-25

Friend, my old friend,
I am sick and still getting sicker.
No idea where all this deep hurting came from.
Either wind whizzing by
Over desolate, bare farm fields,
Or, like groves in September,
I'm rained on by alcohol.
My head flaps its ears,
Like birds flap their wings.
The weight of my roves
My neck can bear no more...
Dark man,
Dark, dark,
Dark man
Takes a seat on my bed,
Dark man
Keeps me up all night long.
Dark man
Moves his finger across filthy pages
And muttering over me,
Like a priest over a corpse,
Tells me a story
Of some scoundrel and binger,
Plunging my heart into fright and recoil.
Dark man,
Dark, dark...
«Listen, listen, -
He haws to himself, -
This book has a lot of great
Thoughts and ideas.
This man here lived in the land

Самых отвратительных
Громил и шарлатанов.
В декабре в той стране
Снег до дьявола чист,
И метели заводят
Веселые прялки.
Был человек тот авантюрист,
Но самой высокой
И лучшей марки.
Был он изящен,
К тому ж поэт,
Хоть с небольшой,
Но ухватистой силою,
И какую-то женщину,
Сорока с лишним лет,
Называл скверной девочкой
И своею милою».
«Счастье, — говорил он, —
Есть ловкость ума и рук.
Все неловкие души
За несчастных всегда известны.
Это ничего,
Что много мук
Приносят изломанные
И лживые жесты.
В грозы, в бури,
В житейскую стынь,
При тяжелых утратах
И когда тебе грустно,
Казаться улыбчивым и простым —
Самое высшее в мире искусство».
«Чёрный человек!
Ты не смеешь этого!
Ты ведь не на службе живешь водолазовой.

Of most abominable
Thugs and phonies.
In that land, come the hiems,
Snow is devilishly white,
With snowstorms coming out
To play tag and be merry.
And the man was a deadbeat of some kind,
But definitely the finest of all
Out there.
He was graceful,
A poet on top,
Of a moderate
Yet dexterous talent.
And some woman
Of forty-something years old
He called 'naughty girl',
And his beloved».
«Happiness, - he'd say, -
Is all sleight of mind and hand.
All those helpless, meek souls
Are known to be always wretched.
No big deal
That a lot of pain
Is caused by those phony
And lying gestures.
Whatever the weather,
Whenever you're bored,
When you're mourning or grieving,
Or just feeling down,
Looking happy, soft-hearted, and smiling a lot –
Is the most precious skill one could ever acquire».
«Nasty dark man!
You are out of your mind!
Whatever you want, you will certainly fail.

Что мне до жизни
Скандального поэта.
Пожалуйста, другим
Читай и рассказывай».
Чёрный человек
Глядит на меня в упор.
И глаза покрываются
Голубой блевотой.
Словно хочет сказать мне,
Что я жулик и вор,
Так бесстыдно и нагло
Обокравший кого-то.
. . . .
Друг мой, друг мой,
Я очень и очень болен.
Сам не знаю, откуда взялась эта боль.
То ли ветер свистит
Над пустым и безлюдным полем,
То ль, как рощу в сентябрь,
Осыпает мозги алкоголь.
Ночь морозная.
Тих покой перекрестка.
Я один у окошка,
Ни гостя, ни друга не жду.
Вся равнина покрыта
Сыпучей и мягкой известкой,
И деревья, как всадники,
Съехались в нашем саду.
Где-то плачет
Ночная зловещая птица.
Деревянные всадники
Сеют копытливый стук.
Вот опять этот чёрный
На кресло мое садится,

I don't give a toss
About this poet's life.
Please, just bore someone else
With your fanciful tale».
Dark man
Gazes fixedly at me.
And his eyes get filled up
With pale-blue vomit.
Like he's trying to tell me
I'm a con man and thief,
Who so rudely and boldly
Got somebody burgled.
. . . .
Friend, my old friend,
I am sick and still getting sicker.
No idea where all this deep hurting came from.
Either wind swishing by
Over desolate, bare farm fields,
Or, like groves in September,
I'm rained on by alcohol.
Frosty night.
Streets are empty and dreamy.
I'm alone by the window,
Not expecting a soul to come round.
The landscape is spread
With whitewash so free-flowing and creamy,
And the trees, like horse riders,
Have parked in our yard.
In the distance,
Night crows can be heard singing grimly.
Wooden horse riders jib
To the tireless patter of hoofs.
Yet again the dark stranger
Takes his seat by the window,

Приподняв свой цилиндр
И откинув небрежно сюртук.
«Слушай, слушай! —
Хрипит он, смотря мне в лицо,
Сам всё ближе
И ближе клонится. —
Я не видел, чтоб кто-нибудь
Из подлецов
Так ненужно и глупо
Страдал бессонницей.
Ах, положим, ошибся!
Ведь нынче луна.
Что же нужно еще
Напоенному дремой мирику?
Может, с толстыми ляжками
Тайно придет «она»,
И ты будешь читать
Свою дохлую томную лирику?
Ах, люблю я поэтов!
Забавный народ.
В них всегда нахожу я
Историю, сердцу знакомую, —
Как прыщавой курсистке
Длинноволосый урод
Говорит о мирах,
Половой истекая истомою.
Не знаю, не помню,
В одном селе,
Может, в Калуге,
А может, в Рязани,
Жил мальчик
В простой крестьянской семье,
Желтоволосый,
С голубыми глазами…

Tipping top hat to greet me
And adjusting his casual suit.
«Listen, listen! –
He croaks, looking me in the face,
Leaning to me
Yet closer and closer. –
You're the first perfect douchebag
That I've met,
Who'd so foolishly suffer
From silly insomnia.
Though I may be mistaken!
Full moon, after all.
Perfect setting, indeed,
For a fool like yourself, supposedly.
Maybe you are in luck,
And tonight you will see that "doll",
And you'll read her that stuff
That you're calling high-quality poetry?
Oh, you poets are funny!
I love you to bits.
You're a walking example
Of a story so clichéd and trivial, -
How a pimpled girl-student
Is wooed by a geek,
Who talks of the sublime
While trying to curb his libido.
I cannot recall
In which village it was,
Maybe Kaluga,
Or most likely Ryazan.
A peasant couple
Once had a boy,
So yellow-haired,
With eyes almost cyan…

И вот стал он взрослым,
К тому ж поэт,
Хоть с небольшой,
Но ухватистой силою,
И какую-то женщину,
Сорока с лишним лет,
Называл скверной девочкой
И своею милою».
«Чёрный человек!
Ты прескверный гость.
Эта слава давно
Про тебя разносится».
Я взбешён, разъярён,
И летит моя трость
Прямо к морде его,
В переносицу…
. . . .
…Месяц умер,
Синеет в окошко рассвет.
Ах ты, ночь!
Что ты, ночь, наковеркала?
Я в цилиндре стою.
Никого со мной нет.
Я один…
И разбитое зеркало…

In due course he matured
And turned a bard,
Of a moderate
Yet dexterous talent.
And some woman
Of forty-something years old
He called 'naughty girl'
And his beloved».
«Nasty dark man!
You're a foul thing.
You have long been ill-famed
For your antics and lies.»
I'm pissed off, outraged,
And I'm thrusting my stick
Into his evil face,
Right between the eyes…

. . . .
…The moon's died,
And the window is lit up by dawn.
Evil night!
Why are you now a hazard?
Top hat still on my head,
I'm completely alone.
It's just me…
And the mirror – all shattered…

Быть поэтом — это значит то же,
Если правды жизни не нарушить,
Рубцевать себя по нежной коже,
Кровью чувств ласкать чужие души.

Быть поэтом — значит петь раздолье,
Чтобы было для тебя известней.
Соловей поет — ему не больно,
У него одна и та же песня.

Канарейка с голоса чужого —
Жалкая, смешная побрякушка.
Миру нужно песенное слово
Петь по-свойски, даже как лягушка.

Магомет перехитрил в коране,
Запрещая крепкие напитки,
Потому поэт не перестанет
Пить вино, когда идет на пытки.

И когда поэт идет к любимой,
А любимая с другим лежит на ложе,
Благою живительной хранимый,
Он ей в сердце не запустит ножик.

Но, горя ревнивою отвагой,
Будет вслух насвистывать до дома:
"Ну и что ж, помру себе бродягой,
На земле и это нам знакомо".

"Poetry is always masochistic..."
From the cycle of poems 'Persian motifs', 1925

Poetry is always masochistic,
Stating facts of life without caution.
Poets can't help being agonistic -
Words they spout are bleeding with emotion.

Poetry is singing one's heart out,
Making everyone around affected.
It is natural to them, no doubt.
Birds don't think – their songs are self-directed.

Mockingbirds have never been respected -
Little silly errors of their species.
No one needs a song that's been perfected.
Poets sing their minds – that's why they're precious.

Many men of wisdom acted clever,
Damning liquor to divert attention.
Yet they loved their wine and they knew better:
Wine can heal all those who are in anguish.

If so happens that our rhyme maker
Catches out his darling with a lover -
Comforted and soothed by the sweet nectar,
Never will the poet grab a dagger.

He will wander off, engulfed by passion,
Crooning to himself a kind of prayer:
'Well, so what of it? I'll die a swagman.
Knowing life, I might say I'm prepared.

"Несказанное, синее, нежное…", 1925

Несказанное, синее, нежное…
Тих мой край после бурь, после гроз,
И душа моя — поле безбрежное —
Дышит запахом мёда и роз.

Я утих. Годы сделали дело,
Но того, что прошло, не кляну.
Словно тройка коней оголтелая
Прокатилась во всю страну.

Напылили кругом. Накопытили.
И пропали под дьявольский свист.
А теперь вот в лесной обители
Даже слышно, как падает лист.

Колокольчик ли? Дальнее эхо ли?
Всё спокойно впивает грудь.
Стой, душа, мы с тобой проехали
Через бурный положенный путь.

Разберёмся во всём, что видели,
Что случилось, что сталось в стране,
И простим, где нас горько обидели
По чужой и по нашей вине.
Принимаю, что было и не было,
Только жаль на тридцатом году —
Слишком мало я в юности требовал,
Забываясь в кабацком чаду.
Но ведь дуб молодой, не разжёлудясь,
Так же гнётся, как в поле трава…
Эх ты, молодость, буйная молодость,
Золотая сорвиголова!

"Indescribable, blue, tender-hearted...", 1925

Indescribable, blue, tender-hearted.
My land peaceful again after storms.
And my soul – like a boundless plough field –
Breathes aromas of honey and rose.

I've calmed down. Years have slowly engrossed me.
Yet I'm not hating what has been.
Like a trio of wild Russian horses,
I raced past me, quick as the wind.

Dust and mud are what's left of my passage,
And a devilish whistle far off.
All around is so quiet and placid
You could hear the smallest pin drop.

Soothed by distant ding-dong of the ages,
I have learnt to take things as they come.
There, soul, we have neared the edges
Of our turbulent, thorny path.

Let's recap what we've seen and experienced,
And what's happened to our sweet home.
Let's forgive those who wronged or insulted us,
Through our own or through their fault.
I accept what has been and what hasn't been,
At the threshold of thirty years -
I just wish I had not been so in-between,
And avoided the tavern fumes.
But then even an oak tree, just planted,
Can give way, like new grass in the wind...
Oh, my youth, my unstoppable callowness,
A wild child with a golden head!

"До свиданья, друг мой, до свиданья...", 1925

До свиданья, друг мой, до свиданья.
Милый мой, ты у меня в груди.
Предназначенное расставанье
Обещает встречу впереди.
До свиданья, друг мой, без руки, без слова.
Не грусти и не печаль бровей.
В этой жизни умирать не ново,
Но и жить, конечно, не новей.

"Good-bye, my friend, it's time to leave…", 1925

Goodbye, my friend, it's time to leave.
My dear, you are in my heart.
The parting that was meant to be
Promises we'll meet, somehow.
Goodbye, my friend, no hand, no sigh.
Goodbye, my friend - and, please, don't grieve.
In this life it is not new to die,
Much more is it common to live.

Кто я? Что я? Только лишь мечтатель,
Перстень счастья ищущий во мгле,
Эту жизнь живу я словно кстати,
Заодно с другими на земле.

И с тобой целуюсь по привычке,
Потому что многих целовал,
И, как будто зажигая спички,
Говорю любовные слова.

"Дорогая", "милая", "навеки",
А в уме всегда одно и то ж,
Если тронуть страсти в человеке,
То, конечно, правды не найдешь.

Оттого душе моей не жёстко
Ни желать, ни требовать огня,
Ты, моя ходячая берёзка,
Создана для многих и меня.

Но, всегда ища себе родную
И томясь в неласковом плену,
Я тебя нисколько не ревную,
Я тебя нисколько не кляну.

Кто я? Что я? Только лишь мечтатель,
Синь очей утративший во мгле,
И тебя любил я только кстати,
Заодно с другими на земле.

"What am I? I'm just a fantast...", 1925

What am I? I'm just a fantast,
Searching for the sunshine in the fog.
I have lived this life only in passing,
Joining all the others on this earth.

Kissing you is nothing but a habit,
For I've done a lot of that before.
Words of love I utter have no merit,
They just spark and die, like fireworks.

All those "Darling", "sweetheart" and "forever",
But the same thing's always on my mind.
When one has to deal with human fervours,
Truth is just impossible to find.

That is why it doesn't really hurt me
To pine for or clamour for your treats.
You, my lovely, graceful birch-like pippin,
Were once made for many and for me.

Deep inside, though, I am always waiting
For that special someone, my soul mate.
So of you I'm never really jealous,
Nor have I been known to call you names.

Who and what am I? Only a fantast,
Who has lost his dreamboat in the fog.
And –alas – I loved you just in passing,
Joining all the others on this earth.

'I AM JUST WHAT I AM': ESENIN IN QUOTES

According to linguistics, the best way to understand a nation is to look closely at its language. Language is the best reflection of a nation's mentality, and by studying how a certain language evolves one can more or less understand what social, cultural, or economic changes a given society has been undergoing; or what is at the core of a nation's individual and global consciousness.

Traditionally, Russian culture does not operate in terms of understatement and sugar-coating. Subconsciously, these are seen as dishonest and insincere. Both are things that are not tolerated by the Russian soul.

At the same time, Russian directness and spontaneity go hand in hand with naivety which at times borders on foolishness – which is never a good combination! Often perceived as a weakness in the West and therefore periodically abused, Russian naivety comes from inner conviction, reflecting millennia of ancient Slavic heritage, that others simply cannot be acting dishonestly towards us, as we wouldn't do so to others. What you see is what you get with Russians. I would even go as far as to say that intolerance to hypocrisy and insincerity is in our genetic blueprint.

Here again, Esenin is a great example of this national trait. He simply could not stand hypocrisy and lies; even the slightest insincerity of manner irritated him. He would always try and expose it, giving little thought to how hurt others might feel as a result.

Ilya Schneider once witnessed a row Esenin had with Isadora over a dinner table. He had just told Schneider how uncomplimentary Isadora had been about him on their foreign travels: calling her Soviet impresario names and accusing him of exploiting her talent. It naturally frustrated Esenin to see how Isadora fawned over Schneider upon their reunion in Moscow. Isadora, in turn, tried to pass the accusation off as a lie, which Schneider never believed. In his memoirs, he wrote of that incident: "Isadora tried to convince us that Esenin had misunderstood her, but I was quite sure that what Esenin had told us was true."

Considering Esenin's innate inability to lie, pretend out of politeness, or cosy-up, some of his infamous traits begin to look less scandalous and may even be seen as something different altogether: his rudeness as outspokenness; bad language as a distress call; later cynicism as resentment of the gruesome post-revolution reality.

Please meet a Esenin that is rarely, if ever, mentioned in Russian literature textbooks: a sweet yet shameless straight-talker – as portrayed in his own quotes.

***

"My dear Ilya Ilyich, why does he write poetry? Tell him not to."

***

"I live roughly, somehow, without a place I can call my own, because at home I am constantly disturbed by all sorts of good-for-nothing loafers…<> I simply don't know how to get rid of these stupid fools and I'm getting thoroughly ashamed of burning the candle at both ends."

***

"For everything, for everything, for everything, for everything I thank you…!"

***

"They say I write without making corrections. Sometimes there are corrections. I do not write with a pen. I merely put the final touches on with a pen."

***

"Isadora hated the Russian Tsarist Regime. So did I. Always. I was even punished for it and sent to join a penal battalion."

***

"My fellow poets were carried away by the figurativeness of the verbal form. They seem to think that the word and the image are one and the same thing."

***

"I'm sick to death! Another time. To hell with them!"

***

"When committing suicide, the Japanese cut open the stomach with the large knife and when the bowels fall out cut off the last gut with the little dagger. What self-control and what barbarity!"

***

"Did I raise hell there because I was drunk? Was it so bad? I raised hell for our revolution!"

***

"Germany? We'll talk about it later, when we meet, but it isn't much of a life here. Life is in our country. There is really the slow, sad decline here that Spengler talks about. We may be Asiatics, we may have a bad smell, we may scratch our bottoms shamelessly in public, but we don't stink of putrefaction as they do.

There can be no revolution here..."

***

"The strength of reinforced concrete, the enormous bulk of the buildings, have compressed the brains of the American and narrowed his sight. The customs of the Americans reminded me of the never to be forgotten customs of Ivan Ivanovich and Ivan Nikiforovich in Gogol's story. Just as for the heroes of Gogol's story there was no better city than Poltava, so for the Americans there is no better and more civilised country than America. 'Listen,' an American said to me, 'I know Europe. Don't argue with me. I have been all over Greece. I saw the Parthenon. But all that is not new to me. Do you know that in the state of Tennessee we have a much better and a much newer Parthenon?' Such words make one wish to laugh and to cry at the same time."

***

"Now, what if there weren't any cows? No, no. Without cows there would be no villages, and one can't imagine Russia without villages."

"Is not sensuality part of a powerful and real love? Are we walking on clouds and not on the earth?"

***

"I do not recognise any language except Russian, and if anyone wants to talk to me, he'd better learn Russian."

***

"My lyrics are animated only with my great love for my country."

ESENIN AND OUR TIME

Being a life-long fan of Sergei Esenin's talent and philosophy, naturally, I often think what he might have to say about things if he were reincarnated today.

He might have been rather surprised to learn that all was not doom and gloom during the Soviet rule which he had come to loathe towards the end of his life. He might have even felt proud to know that (under the controversial reign of Joseph Stalin) his beloved nation had defeated fascism, made an enormous industrial leap forward, and built (for a little while) a near-perfect socialist empire with unrivalled free healthcare, housing, and education.

He would have been thrilled to watch footage of the first Soviet spaceship darting towards outer space and to realise that all future space exploration was only made possible thanks to the Soviets' sheer, against-all-odds ingenuity and enthusiasm; something he himself had not been deprived of.

He would have been bemused by the mishmash of

data littering people's minds daily. And he would have certainly regarded our attachment to smartphones and technology as a sign of a mental disorder, which may not be far from the truth.

He might have been rather skeptical of what is defined as fine art and fine literature today, and might have disapproved of how far society has gone in adapting, transforming and substituting once classic and seemingly unshakeable human values.

Neither would he have approved of the global dominance of the English language, and the poor state of his mother tongue, infiltrated with English words and occasional monstrous hybrids.

But the one thing he would have definitely rejoiced in would have been to know that his name is up there, next to Alexander Pushkin's in the paradigm of Russia's most venerable poets. And that his unconditional love for his Motherland is not lost on his descendants, shining through his every line, making his persona a poetic manifestation of the truly Slavic, *Russian* identity for centuries to come.

BIBLIOGRAPHY

'Любовь и смерть Сергея Есенина', Издательство Дефант, Москва, 1992. (Collected memoirs by Ilya Schneider, Isadora Duncan, and Eduard Khlystalov)

Schneider, Ilya Ilyitch. Isadora Duncan: The Russian years. Translated by David Magarshack. Macdonald & Co; 1st ed. Edition, 1968.

Irma Duncan and Alan Ross Macdougall, 'Isadora Duncan's Russian Days and her last years in France', Victor Gollancz LTD, 1929; digitized by the Internet Archive in 2016 (https://archive.org/details/isadoraduncansru00dunc)* –97 – 102

Sukhih, I.N., 'Russkaya literatura dlya vseh. Klassnoe chtenie! Ot Bloka do Brodskogo – Lenizdat, 2017. (https://profilib.net/chtenie/35381/igor-sukhikh-russkaya-literatura-dlya-vsekh-klassnoe-chtenie-ot-bloka-do-brodskogo-58.php)*

Есенин С. А. Полное собрание сочинений в 7 томах. — М.: Наука; Голос, 1997.

Alexandra Guzeva. Skyscrapers, poverty and the power of the dollar: Things that impressed Russian writers in the U.S. Russia Beyond, 2017 https://www.rbth.com/history/326273-what-impressed-russian-writers-america*

Annotated poems http://www.esenin-sergej.ru/esenin/text/stihi-kommentarii/kommentarii-14.php*

* The web addresses referenced in this book were live and correct at the time of the book's publication but may be subject to change.

DID ESENIN'S POETRY STRIKE A CHORD?

If so, please share your thoughts (#MyEseninBook)

Olga is a London-based freelance translator and copywriter who thrives on her international East-meets-West DNA. She was born in Western Siberia, USSR, at the turn of the decade that would prove a testing time for the generation of her parents and peers alike. Despite the meagre teacher salary, Olga's mother had gone to great lengths to secure the best education for her daughter at the Nevsky Institute for Language and Culture in St Petersburg, Russia, where Olga spent five years majoring in English, French, and the Theory of Translation. She graduated on top of her class with an academic accolade featuring a study allowance from a regional division of Gazprom, and a scholarship at Cambridge University. When she's not chasing doggies and birdies with her toddler in a park, Olga can be found rereading books by English thriller writer James Hadley Chase, binge-watching Ghost Adventures, or clicking away at her old typewriter-inspired keyboard.

Printed in Great Britain
by Amazon